The Authentic Lover

The Authentic Lover

Reclaiming Love's Beauty and Power

Chris Hakim

© 2017, 2023, 2026 by Chris Hakim. All rights reserved. No part of this publication may be reproduced, distributed, or transmitted in any form or by any means, including photocopying, recording, or other electronic or mechanical methods, without the prior written permission of the publisher, except in certain other uses permitted by copyright law.

Wise Love Books

10 9 8 7 6 5

Permissions:

The Book of Five Rings, by Miyamoto Musashi, translated by Thomas Cleary, ©1993 by Thomas Cleary. Reprinted by arrangement with The Permissions Company, Inc., on behalf of Shambhala Publications Inc., www.shambhala.com.

Shambhala: The Sacred Path of the Warrior, by Chögyam Trungpa; © 1984 by Chögyam Trungpa. Reprinted by arrangement with The Permissions Company, Inc., on behalf of Shambhala Publications Inc., www.shambhala.com.

ISBN 978-0-9981553-0-2 (trade paperback)
ISBN 978-0-9981553-1-9 (eBook)

1. Body, mind and spirit / sacred sexuality   2. Family and relationships / love and romance   3. Sex and sexuality: advice and issues   4. Religion / sexuality and gender studies   5. Psychology / human sexuality   6. Social science / human sexuality

204.4 H164a
HQ31.H164 2025
LCCN 2016915779

Fire whispers in smoke's ear:
"The aloeswood does not complain.
It knows my worth and thanks me.
From its own annihilation,
It fulfills its purpose!"

Rumi, *Divan-e Shams*

Contents

Introduction

Part One: Violence and Gentleness
   1. The extent of the problem   11
   2. Take ownership of your state of mind   15
   3. Lovemaking: reversing ancient habits   25
   4. Ho'oponopono: the Hawaiian forgiveness ritual   27
   5. Gentleness: the poise of the tiger   32
   Contemplations   34
   Pledge   35

Part Two: Pettiness and Grace
   6. Our petty, deadly sins   39
   7. Overcoming pettiness   52
   8. Courtly love   56
   9. How to kiss like in the movies   67
   10. Lovemaking: a preliminary exercise   70
   11. Gracious love: the bouncy snow lion   73
   Contemplations   74

Part Three: Vanity and Charm
   12. What is attractiveness?   77
   13. The problem of the peacock   82
   14. Approaches to overcoming vanity   87
   15. The *ahal* of the Tuareg   93
   16. The peacock redeemed   100
   17. The outrageous charm of the garuda   103
   18. What's all this tantric stuff, anyhow?   106
   19. How to make love   113
   Contemplations   118

Part Four: Agenda and Mystery
- 20. The last great enemy — 121
- 21. Everyone's agenda — 126
- 22. The purpose of sex — 137
- 23. Beyond the agenda — 142
- 24. Four mysteries of love — 145
- 25. The way of the samurai — 148
- 26. Magical practices — 158
- 27. The mysterious dragon — 164
- Contemplations — 167
- Consecration — 169
- Aspiration — 174
- Notes — 175
- Index — 179
- Bibliography — 183

Introduction

> In youth, man does not understand the Tao. At middle age he hears much about the Tao but does not practice what he hears. When he is old he sees the truth of Tao, but is too weak to act on it.
>
> — Sun Simiao, 6th century Chinese physician

This is a magical book. It will transform you, if you will let it. It is not a self-help book, which promises to take you from *here* to *there*. That would depend on what *here* and *there* mean. The goal is not to adopt the *one correct way* to love, because there is no such thing. This is also not a very orthodox book, because it aims to undermine a number of preconceived ideas more or less all of us have. And we cling to those ideas as if our lives depended on it, in spite of that not making us happy.

The main thesis is that within sexual relations, love is beset by four great enemies. They are, from the grossest to the subtlest, *violence, pettiness, vanity,* and our *reproductive agenda*. Those are not external enemies but internal ones, psychological quirks and ingrained mental habits. Out of fear, confusion, or habit, we have convinced ourselves that a small or large dose of them is necessary for our survival. Without them, we feel naked, unbearably vulnerable. Yet it is this very vulnerability that is required to enter into a deep communion with another person. Those obstacles, which we impose on ourselves, not only do not procure happiness, but are problematic. A number of practices, some ancient and traditional, some made up for the purpose at hand, are suggested as ways to mitigate and perhaps overcome those great enemies.

Introduction

Of the four great enemies, violence is the most obvious. It stems from a purely physical or materialistic approach to sexuality and reproduction, a state of complete alienation from the spirit. Pettiness is the most prevalent. It is a preoccupation with one's emotional and mental comfort, and the false but widespread idea that love is nothing but an emotion, rather than something that captures our entire being. Vanity is the most intractable. It is the compelling desire for an attractive mate. It is present in most, and perhaps all cultures, but living in a consumerist society exacerbates it. Our reproductive agenda, the most insidious, is our tendency to obey our reproductive instincts (and sometimes those of others), without regard for the ensuing happiness or misery of ourselves and others.

Overcoming the enemies of love gives rise to four respective virtues of *gentleness, grace, charm,* and *mystery*. Those four names are simply placeholders for rather large ideas of the progressive liberation of the mind; freeing the mind of ingrained habits will be discussed at length. For example, it is obvious violence is to be avoided. But the kind of gentleness we are looking for is not merely refraining from behaving violently. It is the pacifying of our tendency to resort to hurtful expedients, whatever they may be. We can cultivate gentleness to the point we feel confident we can conduct our love life (better, our entire life) without the slightest meanness, deception, or any other shortcut.

This alone would be a remarkable achievement, quite out of the ordinary, for even when we act in the most civilized manner we usually harbor violent thoughts. Likewise grace, charm, and mystery are non-obvious qualities, which reflect further and further refinement, and a greater and greater capacity for love, free of undesirable baggage. By renouncing pettiness, we allow ourselves the luxury of ethical living, always concerned about others, and personally embodying the larger view of the society we want to live in. Going beyond vanity, we then further extend our vision and discover our innate charm: we do not need to *act* charming or make ourselves pretty or suave. Finally, we may discover the timeless mystery of unconditional love, beyond any reproductive or other agenda.

We eventually find out that these qualities are not cultivated; they were with us all along, but buried in our habitual ways of thinking and acting. We are not making anything up; the virtues of authentic love are inherent, and dawn on us as a recollection of sorts. It is strangely satisfying to rediscover the goodness we are all born with, but then forget along the way.

It is no accident these virtues resemble the *four dignities* of Shambhala, a Buddhist-inspired tradition of spiritual warriorship: meekness, perkiness, outrageousness, and inscrutability. They are an integral part of the tradition in which I grew, and will be referred to by way of analogy. But it is my wish that non-Buddhist readers also benefit. Hopefully, readers can make adjustments to their respective spiritual or religious traditions. For this reason, I have tried to write this book free of Buddhist jargon. As much as possible, I have tried to show that the pursuit of a gentle and dignified human life does not belong exclusively to any one culture. It is rather a shared human heritage, present in many places, a common human concern. Therefore, to the extent I was able to understand them, I have cited from other traditions too.

INTRODUCTION

This book is not the work of a professional, but the result of a personal quest, often a painful struggle, over many years. As a young man living in Los Angeles at the time, having grown up in a more innocent culture, I was time and time again shocked at the superficiality and self-delusion prevalent in the *singles scene*. It seemed straightforward and justified to write a book about a more sensitive or spiritual approach to love and sex. *Just relax and be yourself*, I thought of writing. At the time I only had a vague idea of what spirituality meant. Was it simply a matter of having a generally liberal attitude and hoping for the best?

As I was to discover over the following three decades, human sexuality is a painful and tightly-wound puzzle, the Gordian Knot of human existence as it were, but ultimately not an impossible challenge. After all this time, I have found the clarity and vantage point to write something I hope will be helpful. Maybe it took so long because I am slow to come to conclusions, and also because I spent so much time in fruitless avenues. This would have been quite foolish, but for the hope of saving another from learning by trial and error. As Otto von Bismarck famously said, only a fool learns from his own mistakes. The wise man learns from the mistakes of others.

The first encounter I had with a spiritual form of sexuality was through Mantak Chia's *Taoist Secrets of Love* shortly after it came out. It is now a classic of the genre, now republished as the more commercial *Multi-Orgasmic* series. In it the author describes at length the benefits of withholding ejaculation during sex. A companion book authored by Chia and his wife Maneewan Chia, *Healing Love Through the Tao* is also available, and describes comparable practices for women. The idea, rather unknown in the West, is well-known to some Taoist practitioners and to proponents of so-called tantric sexuality. As it was my good fortune to have an early exposure to this practice and to explore its physiological, psychological, and ethical ramifications, I came to see it as the potential basis for a form of spirituality, beyond mere technique. Bodily discipline alone does not make for spiritual practice. For spirituality proper, I am indebted to the Buddhist tradition, and especially the Shambhala teachings, which Chögyam Trungpa brought to the West from Tibet.

Beyond the need for personal discipline, a good deal of realism is necessary to approach sexuality. It is not obvious to adjust our attitude realistically between rank cynicism and wishful thinking. On the one hand, we intuit humans have a vast potential for love and selflessness. On the other hand, we seem to have an equally limitless capacity for meanness and selfishness. We need to anchor ourselves in objectivity, and for this reason I rely on science for facts, rather than on wishful thinking, popular ideas, or religious dogma. The modern science of evolutionary psychology and its precursor ethology shed much-needed light over previously incomprehensible aspects of our behavior, and sexual behavior in particular. Here is what Professor David Buss writes at the start of his *Evolution of Desire*:

> Pain, betrayal and loss contrast sharply with the usual romantic notions of love... Discord and dissolution... are thought to signal personal inadequacy, immaturity, neurosis, failure of will, or simple poor judgement in the choice of a mate. This view is radically wrong. Conflict in mating is the norm and not the exception.

Introduction

The chief role of science is to discover facts with as much clarity and objectivity as possible, where our personal biases might otherwise interfere, especially facts we are not inclined to accept. But the ways of science are not geared toward prescribing behavior, other than the very obvious. The choices we make in our lives are a matter of conscience and not of science: they depend on our values, and on what we want to accomplish. That is why philosophy and spirituality can offer guidance, beyond the raw facts. Thus there no need for any contradiction between science and religion or philosophy, if we keep each in its proper place.

We are in a real mess, yet we believe in love, and hold it to be so valuable as to accept the risk of failure and its associated costs. We try our luck. We persist even after many failures, distractions, and dead ends. Is having a good or bad experience with love just a matter of our own luck, such as finding the right partner? If we must believe David Buss when he states that conflict is built into human mating, then a form of conflict management is obviously in order. First, we must set the facts down thoroughly. This requires honesty. Next we approach our options with a view conducive to happiness. We can obtain such guidance from our spiritual or religious background, or from secular philosophy or ethics. In a non-theistic tradition such as Buddhism, the spiritual path means seeing the world as it is. With clear seeing, one can engage the world without prejudice or personal baggage. This is not incompatible with science in any way. Thus our ability to enter into meaningful love affairs depends on being free of the mental obstacles that would prevent such clarity.

INTRODUCTION

On the one hand, we have an ancestral mess with no obvious solution at hand. On the other, we tenaciously and irrationally believe in love. Such irrationality is simply an expression of an inalienable faith in our humanity, even as we face evidence to the contrary. Amidst conflict and failure, it represents our desire to achieve the fullest measure of our humanity. Such heroic belief has occurred many times before, in many situations, even when large obstacles loomed. Our persistence helped us overcome seemingly insurmountable odds. Such is the human spirit.

> Almost everything you do will seem insignificant,
> but it is important that you do it.
>
> — M.K. Gandhi

Rather than approaching this book as an authoritative resource, you are invited to reflect: does violence lead to happiness for a long time? What is my part in it? Is gentleness, as described, worth pursuing? If so, to what extent? Are there alternatives? We can decide to cultivate gentleness, and go further into grace, charm, and mystery in the spirit of courageous exploration, as our inspiration will have it. This book is a mere scaffolding of ideas, a roadmap. It does not spell out every possible situation. It is up to you. You can decide to expand, or not, on any of the topics presented. There is no single, correct way. No one can walk the spiritual path for another.

Mountain View, California, December 2016

Part One
Violence and Gentleness

Violence and Gentleness

> One must begin with the realization of pain, duhkha, suffering. Then having realized duhkha, one goes on to the origin of suffering and the path leading out of suffering and liberation. The Buddha did not begin by teaching the beauty of the enlightenment experience.
>
> — Chögyam Trungpa, *Cutting Through Spiritual Materialism*

1. The extent of the problem

Much ink has been spilled extolling the beauty of love. When we think of love and sex, we think about pleasure, tenderness, deep communication, and intimacy. How do we obtain that? We must start not from utopia, but from where we are. Sexuality is fraught with violence, so this is where we must begin.

And we need not look very far. For instance, we may think of rape as a problem of human rights, or of law enforcement, or of education, or as a cultural problem of gender equality. But we do not really want to look at this problem too closely or too personally. We may prefer big sociological abstractions, but rape is actually a very pervasive ill. A study by the psychologist Neil Malamuth found that 35% of college men "indicated some likelihood of raping" if they "could be assured of not being caught." And it is not just a modern problem. In many traditional societies rape is common also.

Although the prevalence of rape is shockingly high, it is far from being the only form of reproductive violence. There are many other forms of violence associated with reproduction and intimacy. The dictionary definition of sexuality is "capacity for sexual feelings… a person's sexual orientation or preference… sexual activity." This definition is strictly limited to sexual feeling and activity. In order to develop a broader insight into human sexuality, it is necessary to broaden the meaning of the word to all those aspects of our behavior, feelings and attitudes relating to our reproduction, such as choosing a mate, courtship, deciding to stay in a relationship or not, conceiving, parenting, marriage, divorce, and so on. Within this larger realm of human reproductive behavior lies a vast range of activity greatly at odds with the expectation of love and everlasting happiness. A lot of marriages end in divorce. Those marriages that do not end may or may not be happy ones. Even after divorce, bitter custody fights often result in innocent children being caught in the crossfire, or losing one fit, loving parent. Since time immemorial, some men have lied to women about love and marriage in order to sleep with them. Domestic violence is yet another common occurrence. In modern society it is more or less equally divided between men and women.[1]

Some women lie to men about their fertility or their use of birth control in order to become pregnant, thus forcing non-consenting men to father children. An informal survey revealed that forty-two percent of the surveyed women would "lie about contraception in order to get pregnant, in spite of the wishes of their partner."[2,3] Some of those women, not content to have forced fatherhood on their partners, add insult to injury by pursuing child support from the alienated fathers. Family courts routinely hold men responsible for child support, even if the man did not consent to the pregnancy, for instance: if the woman gave the man oral sex and inseminated herself against the man's wishes; or when an adult woman was convicted of the statutory rape of a minor boy; or if a woman took advantage of an inebriated man. To address the question of a drunken man's competence to give consent, Dr. Lane Layton testified "a man who is intoxicated to the point of losing consciousness is physically capable of having an erection and ejaculation."[4] Violence can also be legal.

Genital mutilation is another form of reproductive violence visited on the young. While usually justified by religion, morals, or hygiene, both male and female genital cutting are evolution's answer to the problem of sperm competition, a violent, nasty affair.[5] Sleeping with someone we do not really like is also a form of violence, both against ourselves and against the other person. And some people are just plain mean, disloyal, or inconsiderate in ways too numerous to mention. We all carry violence to some extent within us in relation to our reproduction. "If anyone of you is without sin, let him be the first to throw a stone…"

Working to reduce and eliminate violence is therefore what is being proposed as the first step toward a spiritual path. The idea of spirituality seems perhaps incongruous. Maybe we just need to protect people from each other with better laws, or better law enforcement, or better education. This may be the case, but those remedies are only expedients. The real source of violence is within us, and only we can change ourselves. If it is love we ultimately want, the law is too blunt an instrument. We need to work on ourselves directly and personally. We might want to blame others, or society, for violence; but we are not passive subjects of our society. We are also citizens. We cannot just wait for society to turn into a utopia all by itself. We can, and must change ourselves.

We must develop gentleness to gradually replace our habitual ways. Since our behavior arises in our mind, we need to be diligent and tame our mind of violent feelings and tendencies. If it seems obvious, ask yourself: When did I last do that?

History has shown us a great many examples of people fiercely committed to living a life of nonviolence. Mohandas K. Gandhi was nominated multiple times for the Nobel Peace Prize. In 1948, the year Gandhi was assassinated, the Nobel Committee, being of the opinion that the Nobel prize should go to a living person, chose not to award the prize for that year, declaring "there was no suitable living candidate," thus paying him a silent tribute. We have been blessed with Martin Luther King Jr., the 14th Dalai Lama, and Nelson Mandela, all Nobel Peace Prize winners. Many others, famous or not, have contributed to a better world. Rather than being wishful thinking, nonviolence is a very serious business, capable of inspiring and leaving a lasting legacy. As for the bad guys, history shows time and again that tyrants and other baddies are never able to create stable situations. They inevitably meet their downfall, and most often are forgotten. Does anyone remembers Emperor Bokassa the First of the Central African Republic?

Gentleness is the cornerstone of the entire path, for all subsequent steps are simply more subtle and profound aspects of gentleness. Some people like to lace their sexual interactions with roughness or sarcasm as a sign of bravado and sophistication. That is just distraction. Any amount of violence, meanness, or deception can drive love away.

2. Take ownership of your state of mind

You may think the world is hostile, and you therefore need to maintain a tough stance in order to survive. By cultivating this attitude you simply develop a thick skin. You cannot feel tenderness or vulnerability for another. In all likelihood this shell has grown out of habit rather than by deliberate choice. In any case, here you are now, encased in a thick armor, unfeeling and unloving. You must somehow reclaim your ability to love as your birthright.

It will not do to demonize the opposite sex, or your own for that matter. In *Demonic Males*, the anthropologists Richard Wrangham and Dale Peterson show how male violence is supported and rewarded by culture, in which both men and women participate. Both men and women are "extraordinarily ready to admire, to love, and to reward male demonism in many of its manifestations." The undoing of such an evolutionary process would require "an untying of both strands, male and female."

You cannot change the world, but you can change yourself. Gentleness might be the courageous thing to try:

> If we could change ourselves, the tendencies in the world would also change. As a man changes his own nature, so does the attitude of the world change towards him. ... We need not wait to see what others do.
>
> — M. K. Gandhi

If you do not take the risk of being more vulnerable, of approaching the world without meanness, deception, or distrust, you will never even know whether the risk was worth taking. Love dies without ever having left the cocoon.

> From the great cosmic mirror
> Without beginning and without end,
> Human society became manifest.
> At that time liberation and confusion arose.
> When fear and doubt occurred
> Towards the confidence which is primordially free,
> Countless multitudes of cowards arose.
> When the confidence which is primordially free
> Was followed and delighted in,
> Countless multitudes of warriors arose.
>
> — Chögyam Trungpa, *Shambhala: the Sacred Path of the Warrior*

The above passage describes the state of the *warrior*, a person brave enough to face his or her own fears and step out of the cocoon of habitual, fear-based tendencies. Such a warrior is raw, vulnerable, and in constant communication with his or her world, without any trace of avoidance or aggression. Developing gentleness does take that much courage. We need to reassure ourselves that the world is not our enemy, and that creating a decent society begins with us as agents of our own lives. We do not need to be cynical, because our embattlement will only create further problems. We dare to take one step out of the cocoon, and another, and another.

Embrace an authentic spiritual tradition

A spiritual approach requires examining every aspect of our being, including the parts we do not like. Yet we go about ignoring the dark side of human sexual behavior, thinking violence is a kind of aberration that doesn't apply to us. But if we ignore our dark side, our spiritual pretensions will be nothing but a pipe dream. An authentic spiritual approach leaves no stone unturned. Facing ourselves fearlessly requires the support of a living and authentic spiritual tradition. You may belong to a religious or spiritual tradition, or you may look for one. Such a tradition, in order to be authentic, must teach its adherents how to be kind.

My religion is very simple. My religion is kindness.

— The 14th Dalai Lama

Another of His signs is that He created spouses from among yourselves for you to live with in tranquility. He ordained love and kindness between you.

— The Qur'an 30:21

A man combs his hair every morning; why not his heart?

— Old Chinese saying

It may be as simple as the above proverb, but it is absolutely important to actually make the effort to train in kindness. One is never too kind.

Mindfulness meditation

In order to free the mind of meanness, anger, or any other violent emotion, the practice of sitting meditation is especially appropriate. The simplest meditation, practiced by Shakyamuni Buddha some 2,500 years ago, is also one of the most potent. Sit and do nothing. Be mindful of your breath going in and out. Nothing happens. After a while the mind, not accustomed to doing nothing, begins to stir. Ideas and feelings come up. The practitioner notices the stirrings, but is not taken by them and gently returns to the practice instead: the breath going in and out, a simple reference point to return to. The point is not to suppress thoughts or emotions, but to bring clarity by noticing what goes on in the mind. This helps settle the internal chatter. An analogy often employed is that of muddy water. One does not fight the mud or try to make it go away. By refraining from stirring it for a while, the water becomes clear and still as the mud settles at the bottom. The revered Buddhist teacher Thích Nhât Hạnh offers these simple instructions:

> Breathing in, I calm my body.
> Breathing out, I smile.
> Dwelling in the present moment,
> I know this is a wonderful moment! ...
>
> Our appointment with life is in the present moment. If we do not have peace and joy right now, when will we have peace and joy — tomorrow, or [the day] after tomorrow? What is preventing us from being happy right now? As we follow our breathing, we can say, simply, "Calming, Smiling, Present moment, Wonderful moment."

Simple as it sounds, this practice is not only for beginners. Thích Nhât Hạnh mentions that many practitioners, including himself, have relied on this easy but important exercise for many decades.

After some time practicing this way, we become more aware of our thoughts and emotions. We are less caught up in our habitual tendencies. As a result, we become better able to act kindly, deliberately, and reasonably, rather than merely reacting to situations. Meditation has been of great benefit in prisons. If meditation can help in such high-pressure environments, how much more so for the rest of us?

In order to develop and sustain a steady practice, it is usually best to seek instruction from a qualified teacher. Such instruction can be found at various religious and secular centers throughout the world.

Nonviolent communication

The psychologist Marshall Rosenberg developed a method of conflict management called *nonviolent communication*. More than just a style of communication, this process has been used successfully to mediate a variety of difficult situations, even armed conflict. It proceeds in four stages of *observation, feeling, identifying need*s, and *making a request*.

The main point about observation is to be free of judgement. A key aspect of the violent approach is the preoccupation with what we perceive as the rightness of our point of view, and the corresponding wrongness of the other's. A dispassionate, objective observation is thus a reversal of a violent mindset's habit, and the beginning of a compassionate approach to conflict management.

We need to develop a manner of expressing how we feel in order to connect with another more fully. Sometimes we think we are expressing our feelings when we really are expressing veiled judgements. For instance, we may say "I feel misunderstood." Even though we say *feel*, this is not really an emotion, but an assessment of how the other perceives us. We must arrive at a way to express our own feelings rather than finding yet another way to focus on the other's wrongness. More to the point, we may say "I feel upset when you say that," and describe a situation without judgement. Inquiry and practice are needed to arrive at a nonviolent expression of our emotions.

The idea of considering the needs of the parties in conflict, rather than being right or wrong, is radical. Throughout our lives, we have been accustomed to seeing that our needs will not be met if we act or fail to act in a certain way. If you do not do this or that, you will be punished, fired from your job, separated from your children, given a spanking, become penniless — whatever the situation may be. In all cases there is an attempt to model behavior by a continuum of possible bad consequences, whereby normal needs will not be met. The approach of nonviolent communication recognizes the fact that humans have normal and natural needs, and that violence is to be found wherever those needs are not met. For instance, Gandhi said that poverty is the worst form of violence. If we broaden our definition of violence, we will have access to more opportunities to practice gentleness.

The various forms of sexual or reproductive violence thus amount to one person depriving another of some legitimate need. Rape amounts to denying someone their need for physical security, autonomy, psychological well-being, and many other things. Imposing a pregnancy on an unwilling father deprives him of the opportunity to make a deeply personal, meaningful reproductive choice, and also deprives him of the many other opportunities he would rather have pursued. This may also deprive a child of a willing and engaged father, with developmental consequences for the child. With casual sex, we ignore our and another's need for deep and meaningful interaction.

The alternative is to have a dialogue in which both parties acknowledge their own and each other's needs, and then try to find a common ground where all needs can be met. A focus on recognizing human needs as legitimate and worth prioritizing can be the basis of a more humane culture.

Finally, we can learn to make a request with wholly positive wording. Rather than say, *If you do not work hard enough, you will be fired*, try for instance: *The success of my business critically depends on your contribution. Let me give you whatever help I can so that we can both enjoy continued prosperity.* This entails not only a change of wording, but also greater humanity, less agitation, and more confidence in a future positive outcome.

Nonviolent communication thus provides an effective tool to train continuously in nonviolence. After some training, we can apply this principle to all the situations of our lives, including our reproductive and sexual behavior. It is entirely possible. As all things of value, nonviolent communication requires effort over time to bring out what it has to offer. The reader is invited to read Rosenberg's book and other resources for a deeper exploration.

Develop respect for celibacy

Since human reproduction is rife with conflict, dealing with another person intimately, even for a short time, is asking for trouble. Avoiding all sexual activity would be quite rational. Yet generation after generation, we mate, live together, share beds, and raise children, sometimes in the face of great calamities, such as war and famine. We at times endure bad marriages for the sake of providing children with the stability they need. Our reproductive drives are extraordinarily compelling, just like the drive to survive. On the evolutionary scale of many generations, the effect of an individual not reproducing is the same as premature death. Therefore, just as we have inherited powerful survival instincts, we also have nearly intractable reproductive urges. It is no surprise that we should cling to our reproduction with the same intensity as if clinging to life itself. How else could we tolerate this misery?

Konrad Lorenz, early Nazi sympathizer,[6] one of the founders of ethology (a precursor to evolutionary psychology), and 1973 Nobel Prize laureate, studied aggression in the animal realm. His research suggests aggression motivated individuals to spread themselves over their habitat. This alleviates competition over a given environment's finite resources. (Some animals live in packs or herds, because of the advantages of group living. The tendency toward conflict is mitigated by cooperation. But there remains the possibility of conflict between neighboring anthills, tribes, and nations. Humans therefore live in a state of tension between cooperation and competition.)

There comes a point in the growth of a population when the individuals are spread out over all habitable territory. The ethologist and behavioral researcher John Calhoun published a seminal article describing the effect of crowding on rat behavior. If there is nowhere to go, aggression manifests as violence rather than as migration.

As of this writing the human population just passed eight billion and is growing at an inconceivable rate. It is not clear whether the Earth can sustain such a large population over the long run, were we to manage its resources wisely, which we do not. Our ancestral tendency to have so many children is now a clear detriment to the world. Our reproductive instincts do not automatically lead to the greater good. If we give our instincts a free rein, we will simply drive ourselves into madness and destruction.

With the advent of widely-available, safe, and unobtrusive birth-control methods, the problem of rampant population growth is potentially solved. Our love lives do not need to be ruled by the fear of unwanted pregnancy. We do not need to feel sex leads to overpopulating the world either, should we be so worried. But birth control is fundamentally unable to change our innate tendencies. There is no reason why our sexual urges should be any less compulsive, violent, or petty today than they were prior to the advent of modern birth control. Therefore, one option for lessening this preoccupation with sexuality is to embrace celibacy as a form of voluntary simplicity.

> Now to the unmarried and the widows I say: It is good for them to stay unmarried, as I am. But if they cannot control themselves, they should marry, for it is better to marry than to burn with passion... I would like you to be free from concern. An unmarried man is concerned about the Lord's affairs — how he can please the Lord. But a married man is concerned about the affairs of this world — how he can please his wife — and his interests are divided. An unmarried woman or virgin is concerned about the Lord's affairs: Her aim is to be devoted to the Lord in both body and spirit. But a married woman is concerned about the affairs of this world — how she can please her husband. I am saying this for your good, not to

restrict you, but that you may live in a right way of undivided devotion to the Lord.

— *I Corinthians* 7:8–9 and 7:32–35

In the above passage, Paul the Apostle does not speak of sin, of guilt, or of his own moral superiority. He speaks of celibacy as an expedient to free oneself of worldly concerns. If one is especially lustful, he recognizes that "it is better to marry than to burn with passion." Whether to marry is offered as a choice based on the desire to minimize worldly concerns, be those the mundane concerns of householders or the turmoil of unsatisfied passion. A hedonist may argue that sexual passion is spiritual and not worldly. That is putting the cart before the ox. Passion first needs to be purified of violence and other worldly afflictions. The purifying, rather than the passion, can then be claimed as spiritual effort.

As the world population increases and competition for scarce resources increases, concern for "the affairs of this world" is of course becoming more compelling. This in turn accelerates the trend of aggression between individuals and between nations. Our sexual urges are thus intimately linked to aggression and competition over resources. Celibacy is a reasonable, practical choice we can make based on our needs, our situation, and our inclinations.

> When someone brought up the issue of overpopulation, the Dalai Lama said that [by being a monk] he practiced a very gentle form of birth control.
>
> — Barbara Gates and Wes Nisker, *Advice from the Dalai Lama*

This book does not advocate abstinence. But it is worth pausing to consider that it can be a valid spiritual, nonviolent approach. We may find it worthwhile to reflect on our reasons for not being celibate. The option is always open, and it is always helpful to ask ourselves why we cling to our sexuality. Celibacy also at times happens against our wish. When that happens, we can use this opportunity to refrain from the urge to *do something about it*. Celibacy is not a disease that needs to be cured.

3. Lovemaking: reversing ancient habits

Imagine we are free of the urge to reproduce. We can reason ourselves: there is no need for a new baby right now. Are we then motivated solely by the peak of the sexual experience, a moment mere seconds long? William Masters and Virginia Johnson, in their landmark book *Human Sexual Response*, documented what happens in our bodies when we make love. The phases of excitement, plateau, orgasm, and resolution are now well known. This sequence of activity and response revolves around the act of insemination. It is undeniably *natural*. How could humanity have survived if it weren't for this particular form of intercourse? Now when we reach the "resolution" phase, is anything resolved? Is sexual climax a goal worth pursuing? Is it *necessary* to express love? As we detach our lovemaking from our animal urges, we may also be able to reduce our tendency toward violence, cultivate gentleness, and develop a greater capacity to love. This idea is worth exploring.

Dr. Alice B. Stockham was one of the first women to graduate from a United States medical school in the late 19th century, obviously long before the advent of modern contraception. Concerned with the great number of unwanted pregnancies among her patients, she devised a manner of lovemaking with a built-in form of birth control, which she called *karezza*. The method is very simple:

> At the appointed time, without fatigue of body or unrest of mind, accompany general bodily contact with expressions of endearment and affection, followed by the complete but quiet union of the sexual organs. During a lengthy period of perfect control, the whole being of each is merged into the other, and an exquisite exaltation experienced. This may be accompanied by a quiet motion, entirely under subordination of the will, so that the thrill of passion for either may not go beyond a pleasurable exchange. Unless procreation is desired, let the final propagative orgasm be entirely avoided... In the course of an hour the physical tension subsides, the spiritual exaltation increases, and not uncommonly visions of a transcendent life are seen and consciousness of new powers experienced.

Originally devised as a crude form of birth control (if not highly effective, certainly better than nothing at the time), karezza also helped elevate lovemaking beyond physical pleasure and into the spiritual realm. Stockham goes on:

> Karezza gives to the sexual relation an office entirely distinct from the propagative act, a high office in individual development and formation of character. It is both a union on the affectional plane and a preparation for best possible conditions for procreation.

Karezza currently enjoys a following of satisfied practitioners. M. C., happily married for twenty-five years, reports "it creates a deep feeling in a relationship that is very difficult to describe — much deeper than conventional sex." He reports having sex almost every day. "It kind of never ends. Why would I want to give that up for a fifteen-second orgasm?"[7]

In order to bring our reproductive impulses under control, the practice of karezza is suggested here as a middle-of-the-road approach. Neither too lax nor to austere, it requires minimal resolve and provides great spiritual benefits, which can easily be experienced. It also has the potential to cure rampant lust, including the urge to give birth at any cost.

4. Hoʻoponopono: the Hawaiian forgiveness ritual

If you have been wronged, or if you have done wrong and regret it, the *hoʻoponopono* ritual of the traditional people of Hawaii can help heal and transform you to get past the troubling event. Hawaiian culture places a lot of value on the timely restoration of harmonious relationships. Nonviolence is at the heart of native Hawaiian culture. Through a sense of deep connection and interrelatedness, Hawaiians have for centuries maintained and transmitted a culture of gentleness and solidarity:

> The nonviolent society as envisioned by Hawaiians, includes the following essential values integral to the Hawaiian spiritual tradition: a deep reverence and respect for all living objects: *laulima* — working cooperatively together for the good of the community; *pono* — justice, righteousness, and hope; *lokahi* —

harmony in unity; *ho'okipa* — hospitality; *lokomaika'i* — generosity and goodwill; *kokua* — mutual help and cooperation; *'ohana* — extended family, the sisterhood and brotherhood of humanity as central focus of relationships; *aloha 'aina* — love for the land, understanding the interdependence of humanity and the environment; *malama* — caring for each other; *aloha* — the overriding value of love and care for others.

— Paige and Gilliatt, *Nonviolence in Hawaii's Spiritual Traditions*

For maintaining nonviolence within society, a ho'oponopono ritual is employed to resolve conflicts, and to heal grievances and transgressions. Literally, the phrase ho'oponopono means setting right to right, or restoring the natural balance of things, *aloha*. Ho'oponopono has been practiced for centuries as a form of family therapy and more. A respected elder familiar with the process would be invited to help identify and resolve the problem with all interested parties. It would typically involve the extended family and any relevant person. Participants were eager to resolve the problem and took pains searching their hearts for any hard feelings toward others, with a goal of finding lasting forgiveness. Refusing to forgive one who expressed contrition and offered reparation was considered very bad form. Forgiving another also meant letting go of grudges and thus improving one's lot and indeed that of the entire extended family. One Dr. Haertig said "Ho'oponopono may well be one of the soundest methods to restore and maintain good family relationships that any society has every devised."[8]

Morrnah Nalamaku Simeona (1913–1992), whose mother was a native Hawaiian healer and priest was herself recognized as a *kahuna lapa'au* (healer) in Hawaii. She devised and taught her updated version of ho'oponopono starting in 1976. What she taught was intended to bring the spirit of ho'oponopono to a modern and non-native audience. Workshops and seminars are still taught in many countries based on her ideas. Here is her prayer, as reported by her students Joe Vitale and Ihaleakala Hew Len:

> Divine creator, father, mother, son as one... If I, my family, relatives, and ancestors have offended you, your family, relatives, and ancestors in thoughts, words, deeds, and actions from the beginning of our creation to the present, we ask your forgiveness... Let this cleanse, purify, release, cut all the negative memories, blocks, energies, and vibrations and transmute these unwanted energies to pure light. And it is done.

("It is done" is probably the translation of the Hawaiian formula *amama ua noa*, which marks the end of a prayer.) In order to heal from past hurt and violence, in order to let go, you too can perform the modern version of ho'oponopono, four simple steps to forgive oneself and others unconditionally, thereby repairing a damaged relationship between the parties involved and by extension, the rest of the community. We do so from a place of recognition, courage, power, intelligence and peace and search our hearts for our share in the problem, such as specific memories, actions, or judgements. Then, in the spirit of forgiveness, we recite the four magic sentences in earnest:[9]

> **I am sorry.**
> **Please forgive me.**
> **I love you.**
> **Thank you.**

One notable aspect of this process is the complete absence of blame: the perpetrator and the victim do not perform different actions. Either of them, and ideally both together, may perform the ritual to great benefit. In a protracted conflict where the parties have hurt each other a great many times, vast amounts of time and energy are spared by implicitly setting the question of blame aside.

Today, some form of ho'oponopono is encouraged by the criminal justice system of the State of Hawaii:

> In this system, both the offender and victim participate in a type of guided mediation along with other stakeholders in the offense. Ho'oponopono is different from typical mediations because after the session is successfully completed, the participants figuratively cut the "cord" of legal and psychological entanglement that binds them; in other words, the dispute is put to rest forever. When victim and offender come to a true resolution of the problem, and jointly make the decision to move forward without further conflict on the issue, true healing can occur.
>
> — Andrew Hosmanek, *Cutting the Cord*

If you were wronged, what could be the sense of asking for forgiveness? You can ask for forgiveness for seeing the other as less than human, or even as a monster. Anger, no matter how righteous, can only poison you and can hinder healing. Even if you avenge yourself, or the offender is punished lawfully, that outcome will not heal you, and may even create further problems.

> "Tell me, if you buy a gift for someone, and that person does not take it, to whom does the gift belong?"...
> "It would belong to me because I bought the gift."
>
> The Buddha smiled and said, "That is correct. And it is exactly the same with your anger. If you become angry with me and I do not get insulted, then the anger falls back on you. You are then the only one who becomes unhappy, not me. All you have done is hurt yourself... When you hate others, you yourself become unhappy. But when you love others, everyone is happy."
>
> — Jonathan Landaw, *Prince Siddhartha*

While the above story was written for children, adults are not different. Ordinarily we harbor anger with little thought of forgiving, let alone extending love and compassion toward our aggressor. Those four sentences are so simple:

I am sorry. Please forgive me. I love you. Thank you.

It seems ridiculous to think this short prayer should have any power. It is not a magic formula that may or may not have an effect in the future. Theorizing it will not help, will not help. Just try saying it. The miracle lies in your willingness to try it. Even if you feel no inspiration, just take these simple words to heart, for your and the world's sake:

I am sorry. Please forgive me. I love you. Thank you.

5. Gentleness: the poise of the tiger

The unrefined experience of our sexual energy is one of craving, frustration, and conflict. We may satisfy ourselves in such ways as promiscuous, inappropriate, or otherwise unstable relationships; or even long, unhappy marriages. At the root of these expedients lies the desire to service our reproductive tendencies. Our reproduction is seen as a burdensome need. We can alleviate this burden not by constantly seeking gratification, but by cultivating gentleness.

The traditional medical systems of China, India, and Tibet are rich with thousands of years of experience and systematic observation. All three agree that the root of our physical health is our sexual energy. There is a contradiction between sexual energy as basic vitality, and sexual energy experienced as an ongoing state of frustration. After a period of systematic examination, and with the diligent application of whatever practice or practices we choose (meditation, celibacy, karezza, etc.), slowly the do-or-die aspect of our sexual drive subsides. Instead we see great potential, and an opportunity for joy and celebration. Nothing is wrong, nothing lacks, if we are in good health. Even if our health is not perfect, we can still feel a basic wholesomeness about our being. As this realization begins to affect our way of life, we may call this state of being the poise of the tiger. The tiger represents *meekness*, the first "dignity" of the Shambhala tradition of warriorship:

> Meek here does not mean being feeble; it just means resting in a state of simplicity, being uncomplicated and, at the same time, approachable... The analogy for meekness is a tiger in its prime, who moves slowly but heedfully

through the jungle. In this case, the tiger is not searching for prey. He is not stalking in the jungle, hoping to pounce on other animals. Rather, the image of the tiger expresses a combination of self-satisfaction and modesty... From the tip of his nose to the tip of his tail, there are no problems... So his watchfulness is accompanied by relaxation and confidence.

— Chögyam Trungpa, *Shambhala: The Sacred Path of the Warrior*

Such poise, unusual in the conventional world, is available to a kind and dedicated warrior, in love and other aspects of life.

Contemplations

As part of a meditation session, choose one of the topics below and reflect for a few minutes on the question or challenge. However, do not attempt any contemplation that could evoke memories of past traumatic events. Such contemplations *are not and cannot be therapy*. The point is not to find an answer or a solution. It is to bring up the underlying concern, and experience any fear or other emotion as it arises, while sitting in a calm and safe environment. Let yourself experience those feelings and thoughts for a while. Then let go and end with a few more minutes of meditation. Choose a different topic each time.

Is sex a want or a need?

If love is a physical sensation, where is it located?

Imagine having sex with someone whom you do not like.

How would a woman feel if pregnancy were forced on her?

How would a man feel if fatherhood were forced on him?

Imagine living in a household where you are constantly threatened with being separated from your children.

Envision a relationship based on seeing to each other's needs.

Pledge

When you feel ready, you may want to take a pledge, alone or before witnesses, to live a life of nonviolence. Such a commitment helps make the path clearer and leaves no room for regressing. You are embarked on a path of gentleness and bravery, and there is no going back.

I solemnly pledge myself to cultivating gentleness and nonviolence. For the rest of my life, may I respect the needs of others, as well as my own. May I strive to find peaceful solutions to disagreements. May I be gentle and without deceit with my fellow humans in general, and with my intimate partner or prospective partners in particular.

Part Two
Pettiness and Grace

Pettiness and Grace

> Love is patient, love is kind. It does not envy, it does not boast, it is not proud. It is not rude, it is not self-seeking, it is not easily angered, it keeps no record of wrongs. Love does not delight in evil but rejoices with the truth.
> — I Corinthians 13:4–6

6. Our petty, deadly sins

Having reduced our personal, inner violence, we may now be tempted to envision love as an extremely comfortable state, free of disturbance, an ideal emotion, and a great feeling of attachment to another person, which ideally is never frustrated. Pettiness sets in when we begin to think of love as nothing more than mental and emotional comfort, and our entire quest for love amounts to nothing more than avoiding uncomfortable situations. Of course a certain amount of ease is necessary to meet another in full. But it would be a mistake to see comfort, or even emotional satisfaction, as an end in itself.

If we think of love only out of preoccupation with our own comfort, we reduce the ineffability, selflessness, and vastness of love to something familiar, something we can comprehend and control, something smaller than ourselves. A diminished approach cannot inspire, and insisting on it will chase genuine love away. Imagine an old couple who once upon a time were in love, but having worked at their domestic comfort so intently, have lost the deep connection that first brought them together. *And they lived comfortably ever after.*

Not only individuals fall into the trap of pettiness. Pettiness can be agreed upon among members of a group or society. Violence can be reduced or managed to by agreeing to rules, customs, or commandments. But if there is no vision beyond the reduction of violence, that society simply projects a general state of mediocrity. One notes, for instance, that some societies are extremely concerned with their politicians' sexual indiscretions, while other societies not so much. This mediocrity can affect other areas of society as well, if for instance a politician's sex life deprioritizes serious national concerns. A populace given to pettiness is easily manipulated. A petty society does not offer any vision beyond making and enforcing rules, and is not able to foster love among its people. ("Fostering love" here is not all about law or politics. It is not difficult to imagine how love can be expressed as an important value of society through the arts, literature, and the social discourse, as opposed to rules, policies, and laws.)

In order to explore pettiness, and to understand how it came about, let us turn to our ancestral origins. The new science of evolutionary psychology has brought fascinating insights into previously unexplained human behaviors, and reproductive behaviors in particular. Evolutionary reasoning proceeds this way: inheritable behaviors and attitudes that enhanced the propagation of our genes have developed and persisted over successive generations, at the expense of behaviors and attitudes that did not. Such a process of evolution requires no intelligent design, purpose or intention of any sort in order to work. It is deterministic and not particularly moderate or rational. Our inherited tendencies do not need to be conscious, rational, or even ethical, to be experienced as "natural." And while evolution can help explain bad behavior, it does not justify it. We humans must sort out good from bad.

Contrary to the assumption embodied in the popular expression *survival of the fittest* — evolution does not lead to perfect life forms, only to adaptations that ensure optimal survival and reproduction in a given environment. Most importantly, our evolved traits, even those we generally admire, do not necessarily lead us to happiness. The important implication here is that we should not trust our instincts merely because we possess them. We need to have the ability to go against base instincts such as jealousy, possessiveness, and so on. The exploration of what to retain as valuable and what to discard requires courage and the willingness to question our deeply-held beliefs of what is right and proper, and what leads to the greater good of ourselves, of others, and of society. Here is again David Buss in *The Evolution of Desire*:

> The fact that conflicts between men and women originate from our evolved mating psychology is disturbing to some people, in part because it contradicts widely-held beliefs... Evolution operates by the ruthless criterion of reproductive success, no matter how abhorrent the consequences of those strategies may be.

Rather than living out of automatic or habitual thinking, we face the task of discovering the tendencies we have that would cause us to fall into pettiness. The main cause is the pursuit of mental and emotional comfort as a shortcut to real love.

PETTINESS

We need to examine those uncomfortable mental states, and the resulting behaviors, as they occur in our sexual and reproductive lives. It is helpful to start with a simple moral inventory, such as the seven deadly sins of Christianity — wrath, greed, sloth, pride, lust, envy, and gluttony — or the five afflictive emotions of Vajrayana Buddhism — anger, jealousy, passion, pride, and ignorance. We may also discover our own categories of pettiness, based on our individual experience and concerns. The classifications below represent this author's experience, research, and personal reflection. They are offered as indications or hints, rather than as final and categorical. Most of them occur in pairs because they are a byproduct of coevolution, the result of many male-female interactions over numerous generations.

Jealousy, possessiveness, and infidelity

Evolutionary psychology gives us a direct means of analyzing sexual jealousy, this most common of emotions and the source of much tragedy and suffering. We have jealous tendencies because in ancient human (and pre-human) history, those who failed to prevent their mates from straying lost out statistically in the game of reproduction. Male sexual jealousy originates from *paternity uncertainty*, or the inability of a man to be certain he is not raising someone else's offspring. A male is not really harmed by raising another's biological child rather than his own, but evolution favors the genetic line of men who prevented their women, however unpleasantly, from sleeping with other men. We have evolved all sorts of coercive and disproportionate behaviors to discourage women from straying. Such behaviors are often sanctioned by society, and include cloistering, veiling, genital mutilation,[10] violent punishment such as "honor killing," and other quite illiberal norms:

> If a man will be found lying with a woman who is married to a husband, then both of them shall die, the man who lay with the woman and the woman; and you shall remove the evil from Israel.
>
> — Deuteronomy 22:22

The institution of marriage may well have developed solely for the purpose of tracking whose children men are raising.

Paternity uncertainty originates from female promiscuity. There are good reasons to believe ancestral women were not monogamous. One famous marker of such ancient behavior is the size of men's testicles. If only one sperm is needed to fertilize an egg, why incur the expense of manufacturing millions? The answer is that if one woman has sex with several men during her fertile period, the genes of the man who produces the most sperm will be statistically favored. Thus evolution, operating over many generations, has selected those men who produced the most sperm, far in excess of what would be needed absent competition. Conversely, in the animal realm the males of species with monogamous females have smaller testicles relative to their body size.

Now the origin of human female promiscuity as suggested by the evolutionary record is not glamorous either. Available evidence suggests a negative correlation between paternity uncertainty and male infanticide. The male of some primate species will often murder a female's existing offspring in order to make her better able to carry his own. This behavior is all the more prevalent if the male is certain never to have copulated with her.[11] This is also favored by evolution, because those males who murder their rivals' young are at an evolutionary advantage over the less violent males.[12] In species where paternity uncertainty is high, male primates, including humans, are less likely to commit infanticide. Paternity uncertainty is therefore also favored by evolution because it helps reduce infanticide: a man is unlikely to murder a child who is possibly his own. It may be for this reason humans have a tendency to point to physical resemblance of newborns with their fathers, more often than with their mothers.

Women also experience jealousy, but for different reasons. Women feel jealous when men divest material and emotional resources from them, because this means reduced resources for them and their children. Men also have a tendency toward straying because of the obvious evolutionary advantage this behavior confers. This behavior also goes along with the evolved need for female promiscuity. In short, both men and women feel the need to monopolize their partners, and also the need to stray from their partners, but for different reasons. These differences cause misunderstanding between men and women.

Possessiveness manifests as various "mate guarding" behaviors. Some of those have been inventoried by Buss and collaborators in Their *Mate Retention Inventory*:

> Vigilance, concealment of mate, monopolization of time, jealousy induction, punishing mate's infidelity, threats, emotional manipulation, commitment manipulation, derogation of competitors, resource display, sexual

inducements, appearance enhancement, love and care, submission and debasement, verbal possession signals, physical possession signals, possessive ornamentation, derogation of mate, intrasexual threats, and violence against rivals.

Except for "submission and debasement," more common among men, and "violence against rivals," almost exclusively male, the above behaviors are shared rather evenly between men and women. Some of those behaviors, such as "love and care," are benign. Others are obviously detrimental. Out of a surplus of jealousy, we might just suffocate our partner, instead of extending care and respect, as love so rightly requires.

Drama and stonewalling

When we have a dispute with our partner, we may at times tend to escalate the disagreement, using a more and more strident tone, and implying greater and greater emotional urgency, until we get our way. In short, we try to obtain through nagging, emotional display, and histrionics what we cannot obtain through reasoned argument. Both men and women engage in nagging.[13] This approach of course would not exist if it were not successful at least some of the time. There also exists the corresponding tendency to insulate ourselves from our partner's emotional display in order to avoid giving in to their demands. This leads to a vicious circle, where more avoidance leads to more stridency and more emotional behavior leads to more stonewalling. Drama is a subtle form of violence, which has the effect of pressuring the other partner without risking the rapid breakdown of the relationship. In particularly perverse situations, the relationship's value declines to slightly more than nothing and, absent any compelling reason to separate, the relationship goes on limping along for a very long time.

Self-delusion and mediocrity

In Part One, we have noted the intractable quality of our reproductive urges. No matter how awful the situations humans have been in, reproduction has taken place, infallibly, generation after generation, on a very large scale. This infallibility can rightly be called the *law of inevitability*. It is an observed fact that humanity has reproduced, and no doubt will continue to, no matter how wretched the circumstances. If individuals held back and decided not to have children until the situation turns perfect, we would not be around to contemplate this. We have therefore in us a capacity to weather imperfect situations, and specifically imperfect family situations. We might call this the *law of mediocrity*. It is the principle that ensures we stay for a very long time with the same partner, whom we may not really like, but still find vaguely tolerable, even if we have the option to leave and have no children to take care of. No advantage accrues to either party by staying together. They are merely playing out their acceptance of mediocrity.

To make this mediocre situation more acceptable, we also have, necessarily, evolved the capacity to delude ourselves. This is the well-known process of infatuation, which makes us suspend judgment and ignore our partner's faults. We may even call it *falling in love*. But this kind of love faces the pesky problem of *falling out of love*. Love is seen here as a state that befalls individuals, coming and going at various times.

Infatuation may be short-lived. It can also last for two years or so, long enough for a union to produce children, and leave the parents little choice but to raise them. By that time the question of love is, as a practical matter, moot. The evolved tolerance of mediocrity may be all that sustains the family.

Self-abasement and pedestalness

It appears we have a capacity to lower ourselves before our mate in order to retain him or her. Typical behaviors have been identified by Buss and collaborators in their *Mate Retention Inventory*. Such behaviors are more common among men, but not unknown among women:

> He told her that he would change in order to please her.
> He became a slave to her.
> He gave in to her every wish.
> He went along with everything she said.
> He acted against his will to let her have her way.

Again, this behavior could not have evolved if it weren't effective at least some of the time. And for every act of servility, there must be a partner willing to be placed on a pedestal and feel worthy of the offering. It takes two willing parties. Such dualism may be codified and even extolled in society as *chivalry*, *wifely duty*, and other gender-based customs. Moral as they may appear, postures of self-elevation and self-abasement are manifestations of insecurity, and wanting a place in society to secure our reproduction.

Exploitation

Yet another obstacle to love is dwelling on what we feel is scarce for ourselves and for the other. Typically men are seen as having more money and power (whether that is the case or not, and whether earning more actually means controlling and enjoying more wealth). Women are seen as less interested in sex (whether that is true not), and therefore more tightly in control of sex. Scarcity only needs to be felt, not actual, to be a motivation. The obstacle of exploitation is to envision a sexual relationship based on an exchange of what is perceived as scarce, or on the basis of any other type of insecurity. If a sexual relationship has material or emotional insecurity as its basis, it is merely transactional and cannot also be based on real devotion, respect, or tenderness.

Normativeness, hypocrisy, and breaking with tradition

Whenever someone says *I am a man; I am a woman; you are a man*; or *you are a woman*; or when someone says *I am your girlfriend; I am your husband; you are my wife; you are my boyfriend*; etc. trying to resolve a dispute or argument, one may suspect pettiness is at work. By invoking a social norm, imagined or real, we avoid looking at one another more tenderly: what does this person need, what is he or she trying to say?

Predictably, the hatred of non-stereotypical situations, such as male or female homosexuality, gender change, etc. also fits the definition of pettiness. It is more comfortable and fitting, and requires much less mental effort of accommodation, to envision all of society as made up of only two stereotypical, heterosexual genders. Some societies punish homosexuality, even going so far as imposing the death penalty. Such hatred is obviously the opposite of love.

The famous "double standard" makes plenty of sense in light of evolutionary psychology. Nothing in the workings of evolution prevents conflicting and contradictory values. When people marry in a traditional society, women are expected to be virginal and men sexually experienced. How can both sexes comply with such an impossible standard?

Conversely, there also exists a tendency to go against tradition. Rules have been put into place to regulate sexuality, but a lot of people (young people especially) see them as rigid and do not really believe in them. Rules seem impractical and antiquated. Since they often are the mere codification of unconscious behaviors, it is hard to find anyone who can articulate their reason for being. Celibate priests feel qualified to advise their congregants on love, sex, and family. Because of this lack of credibility, it is hard for the young to accept the guidance their tradition would otherwise have to offer. In the modern world, one who follows such rules is easily seen as naïve and missing out on what is going on. Because of that, society is rife with moral relativism and hypocrisy.[14]

Gender-role assignment

One rather developed societal norm is the traditional gender-role division. Men go to work, and women stay home, clean, cook, and raise children. In general, men consciously or unconsciously wanting to control women is the byproduct of paternity uncertainty, and really amounts to controlling women's reproduction.[15] Conversely, there seem to exist instinct-driven societal mechanisms, which function to force men to support their offspring, but only with material resources. We see family courts rabid and ruthlessly efficient about collecting child support from fathers (which mothers rarely have to pay), but often utterly impotent in helping to maintain a meaningful and lasting father-child bond, if not outright hostile. Since minor children cannot be parties in court, the benefit of the children usually attaches to the "custodial" parent in divorce proceedings. By associating women only, rather than both parents, with children, institutions intended for the benefit of children squarely favor women instead. Thus the Massachusetts Department of Social Services was quoted by Stephen Baskerville in *Taken into Custody*: "The best interests of children cannot be separated from the best interests of their mothers," disregarding the importance of fathers in children's lives. Some jurisdictions even force men to pay alimony to women long after they have ceased to be their wives, sometimes for the rest of their lives, altogether bypassing the thin pretext of benefiting children. This can be expected from policies enacted out of vague popular ideas rather than reasoned social discourse.

In summary, there exist instinctual tendencies that tend to favor or restrict one sex or the other in certain arenas of human society. Some of these tendencies manifest as laws or customs. We may think of those as moral and important, or even culturally defining. One the other hand, no one likes to be confined on account of one's gender. Women resent society's attempt to restrict their sexuality (this is often a deep, psychological self-imposition) and to curtail their professional aspirations. Men resent having to support women and being separated from their children. Do we need to treat men and women differently? Vast amounts of research show men and women's psychologies are more similar than they are different.[16] Does society need to take on the task of amplifying gender differences?

In a Buddhist legend, as the bodhisattva Tara almost reached enlightenment, monks advised her to wish for a future male rebirth. It was thought only men could reach full enlightenment. She replied that there is no such thing as *self* or *person* or *awareness*, nor *man* or *woman*. She finally stated "This bondage to male or female is hollow: Oh how worldly fools delude themselves!" She then made a vow to be reborn as a female and reach enlightenment in her female form for all time to come.

Let us not be those "worldly fools" who give so much importance to our gender. This rigidity causes alienation rather than harmony. Instead of dwelling on our differences, let us remind ourselves of our shared humanity, beyond stereotypical gender.

A miscellany of pettiness

Since there is no end to human fallibility, it seems a bit futile to try and describe the manifestations of emotional failings as a finite list of behaviors and attitudes. We could add gossip, idle or malicious; cursing (*breaking the dishes*, figuratively); being always right, or wanting to have the last word; passive-aggressive behaviors; vindictiveness; diagnosing our partner on the basis of made-up or popular psychological ideas; projecting our faults onto the other; self-serving logic; blaming ourselves irrationally; and so on. We are so afraid of our own vulnerability that we will readily cover it up with any comfortable, familiar, or mediocre experience. Intimacy with another human being requires our being vulnerable. In many cases, the obstacle is one of emotional insecurity, and we may simply want to address that problem first. Even just cultivating emotional resilience can help.

7. Overcoming pettiness

> It's a scientific fact. The best way to overcome gravity is with levity.
>
> — Swami Beyondananda (Steve Bhaerman), US comic

To put it simply, one overcomes pettiness by practicing greatness. Greatness is our potential, but it is not given. Some kind of effort is needed. We may be so accustomed to small-scale thinking we may not even know where to begin. First, we need to reflect on the above obstacles, and perhaps other aspects of our lives motivated by small-scale mental or emotional comfort. Then we may think of remedies, just like we remedied our own violence.

Compassion

The disciplines of gentleness in Part One consist mostly in refraining from doing harm. We now extend this gentleness further to the realm of emotions and ideas. Beyond not doing harm, we can also develop a positive discipline of being good citizens, wanting only the good of others, without holding back. This is the practice of compassion.

> Some people consider the practice of love and compassion is only related to religious practice and if they are not interested in religion they neglect these inner values. But love and compassion are qualities that human beings require just to live together.
>
> — The 14th Dalai Lama

In dealing with difficult situations, let us examine our feelings. Does pettiness arise? If we feel threatened or overwhelmed by feeling, chances are we will revert to our primal instincts, which feel most familiar: jealousy, arrogance, withdrawal, the whole gamut. Instead of reacting, let us reflect for a moment. Rather than create a situation of mutual fear and apprehension, here is an opportunity to gain perspective on the other person's point of view. We do not take anything personally. Our feelings probably originate from coevolution and if so, they may have a counterpart in the other person's experience.

Whatever you feel, your spouse feels it too.

— Anonymous

Whatever instinctual behaviors and attitudes we have inherited are the result of the hardships and challenges our ancestors went through long ago. Consider that some of our reproductive behavior and feelings were already in place *before we were even human*. It has been a long, hard road. Let us take a good look at what we are made of and try to sort ourselves rationally. A humanistic, compassionate outlook is necessary to replace our instinctual and conventional behaviors. We need such a counterintuitive effort.

Let us think of great leaders, men and women of high stature whom we respect for their actual greatness, and not just for their fame or social status. What do we admire the most? What makes them different from us? Why could we not be like them? We may think the circumstances of our lives not very significant, but we could also appreciate what we have: our family, our friends, our lover, our coworkers. All of them are significant and worth treating with respect and dignity, as if they belonged to the nobility. Such appreciation is worthwhile and good. It is not self-abasement.

The practice of giving and receiving

Our default tendency is to avoid unpleasant experiences and states of mind, and to cling to pleasant ones. Avoiding unpleasantness prevents us from seeing and relating to the pain and suffering of others. The Buddhist meditation practice of *tonglen*, or giving and receiving, is a powerful method to help develop compassion.

> It is a training in courage, because the whole point of doing it is to train ourselves to be less fearful and anxious… This practice is so extremely beneficial because we're training ourselves to stop thinking about everything from a defensive posture.
>
> — Traleg Kyabgon, *The Practice of Lojong*

Within a session of meditation, we can engage in this practice for five to ten minutes. Ideally, one should first have established a strong practice of mindfulness (breathing) meditation with a skilled instructor. It helps if the instructor is also familiar with tonglen practice. Without that, it is still helpful to know how our mind can be trained away from its usual territorial attitude, and toward selflessness and magnanimity.

> If you want to be miserable, think about yourself.
> If you want to be happy, think of others.
>
> — Tibetan proverb

Instructions for tonglen practice are given thus, breathing in the suffering of others and breathing out whatever ease and comfort we enjoy. Literally, we inhale others' misery and exhale happiness back to them:

> We think of others purely in terms of their suffering and undesirable experiences, imagining the distress of illness, the pain and suffering and loss, the deprivation and affliction of poverty, the confusion and torment of mental illness, and the disabling distress of emotional conflicts. Then we inhale all that suffering into ourselves. We think of ourselves purely in terms of our own happiness, imagining everything that we hold dear, the special moments we cherish when we experienced love or intimacy or moments when we were at ease with ourselves, and we breathe that out to others.
>
> — Traleg Kyabgon, *The Practice of Lojong*

A concern sometimes raised with this practice is whether we might harm ourselves by taking on the suffering of others. We cannot, because it is only a visualization. If our mindfulness practice is strong, those negative feelings dissolve harmlessly in our mind, just like any other thought that might arise in our regular practice. Neither do we deplete ourselves of goodness by extending it to others. We develop confidence and radiance, which in turn inspires others. The more we give, the more we have to give.

Envisioning an enlightened society

Past our meditation sessions, when negative feelings arise in our daily life, we do not shrink from them. Instead we treat them with respect and interest, thinking other people are also experiencing them. We can lean into the discomfort rather than avoiding it. If our tonglen practice is strong, we can project the brave attitude of extending our goodness to others in spite of our own discomfort.

This way we become the ultimate adults, full-fledged citizens who can embrace one another for what we are, instead of being motivated only by the search for comfort. Our view becomes much larger. We can envision a society based on being considerate and compassionate with each other. We first extend our goodness to our circle of friends and to our family. That goodness will eventually be reflected in all of our actions as we envision the world we want to live in. A new couple or a family is a wonderful way to create the society we envision.

8. Courtly love

One major step toward a systematic discourse on love as opposed to marriage or other social norms was taken in Europe from the 12th century, with the literary and social phenomenon of courtly love. Rüdiger Schnell, a professor of literary science and philology, surveyed the characteristics of courtly love, noting its many definitions and contradictions among various sources. The *courts of love* explored the nature of love and the behaviors of lovers, in an attempt to discern the mundane from the exalted. In his view, courtly love aims to set itself apart from other love relations, more banal, as an exceptional form of love.

The courts were asked to resolve disputes between lovers, to clarify the nature of love, or even to decide whether there could be love between married people. The example *arrêt d'amour* (love decision) recorded by the 15th-century French poet and jurist Martial d'Auvergne illustrates the scope and powers of the court:

> The plaintiff, a young woman, said that she had seen her friend to be as joyful and entertaining as could be, well attired, gentle, pleasant, gracious, and agreeable to all... And now he had completely changed and was pensive, moody, and melancholic. He was as if life bored him... If one gave him flowers, he would tear them to bits. As soon as he heard singing or drumming, tears came to his eyes, and he would sigh. If one spoke to him of love at table, he would change the subject to death or bring up some pointless old tale... She requested that the court sentence him to abandoning all melancholic company, and moreover that the court have a provision for him to return to his former state.
>
> In his defense, the poor and sickened lover argued quite to the contrary: the service of Love required many pains and travails, and there was no joy that did not cost a hundred sorrows... As the most loyal of lovers, he was also the most afflicted... In this regard, he had deliberated within himself to abandon all Love... He could only offer his heartfelt thanks to the lady for her good will, but all the same requested that the court grant him leave and license to depart from Love...
>
> When all had been seen and heard, the court ordered the lover to be *mis aux herbes* [literally put out to pasture], and forced to remain in the gardens as a *povre prisonnier* for the duration of one month, so that he would be gladdened at the sight of all the beautiful flowers and greenery. The court forbade him all melancholic company, as well as

walking or daydreaming by himself. The court further ordered the lady to keep him company and spend that month with him to nurse him until he was fully recovered and had returned to his former state.

The sections below model the structure of Schnell's article *L'amour courtois en tant que discours courtois sur l'amour* (courtly love as a courtly discourse on love), except the last. "Privacy and decorum" was added for the needs of this discussion. The point of exploring these characteristics of love is to try and discern a robust ethic, free of unexamined or instinctual bias, and suitable for a wide range of societal needs. A robust ethic means people subscribe to it freely, because it readily makes sense, rather than being imposed a rigid behavioral code only to be discarded when it proves inconvenient. Ethics can be based on reasoned discourse and actual circumstances rather than dogma. Such values would be adapted and adaptable to the needs of the individuals, and help them flourish without constraining them unnecessarily.

Exclusivity

> I cannot share my heart, for in my mind the one who bids for love in two places is a liar and an impostor in each place.
>
> — Arnaut de Mareuil, troubadour (1170–1200)

Is exclusivity required because of intractable jealousy, because of imposed rules, or because of the presumed superiority of an exclusive relation? The answer may be found in the manner in which it takes place. Is it asked for and insisted upon, or is it given freely? The courtly literature is rich with examples of lovers who abjure other romantic pursuits for their true love:

> ... because of the love for a noble lady, towards whom I am attracted and to whom I have given my mind and my heart as token; because for her, I have neglected all the others, so desirable she is to me!
>
> — Bernard de Ventadour, troubadour (1135–1194)

On the other hand, certain laws were formulated by the courts of love, and recorded by Andreas Capellanus. One law states categorically, "3: No one can really love two people at the same time." But the laws of love go on nearly contradicting themselves: "31: Nothing prevents one lady being loved by two gentlemen, or two gentlemen by one lady."

One way to solve this apparent contradiction may be to note the active *loving* in Law 3, versus the passive *being loved* in Law 31. But the need for reciprocity, discussed below, would require that loving and being loved be one and the same. There is still room for debate. Perhaps exclusivity should be offered, but never demanded.

A court of love had even come to the conclusion, as an "irrefragable truth," that love cannot exist between married people, for married people give to each other out of obligation rather than out of love.[17] If exclusivity is a guide rather than a rule, there is still room for *polyamory* (loving more than one person, with the full consent of all the parties) and other explorations. Let love, rather than fixed norms or personal insecurities, be the guide. Out of kindness, let us not arouse jealousy unnecessarily. Let us also be tolerant and trusting of our partner. It will make life that much easier.

PETTINESS

Constancy, sincerity, and lack of self-interest

The values of constancy, sincerity, and lack of self-interest counter the transactional nature of petty arrangements. A relationship based on an exchange will last only as long as each party meets its end of the bargain. The notion of *unconditional love* comes to mind. Love should not be conditioned upon mundane, materialistic, or egoistic concerns. Love absolutely requires authenticity and selflessness. People must be sincere in their pursuit of love as opposed to the pursuit of personal gratification:

> Ah God! If one could distinguish sincere lovers from the fakes, and if flatterers and cheats wore horns on the forehead! I would have given all the gold and silver in the world, if I had them, for my lady to recognize the sincerity of my love for her.
>
> — Bernard de Ventadour

Lack of self-interest is a desirable quality, but it is hard to emulate. We might talk about a transmutation of the suitor's hardships in the service of love into something abstract, the *ennobling* power of love, as this dialogue suggests:

> "If I sing for you and offer you my services, may I not expect benefits therefrom?"
> "You will have success, do not doubt; you will not remain without recompense."
> "How do you understand it, O noble lady?"
> "That you are more noble, and also full of confidence."
>
> — Albrecht von Johansdorf, Minnesänger (c. 1180–c. 1209)

Reciprocity

The prototype of the relationship of courtly love is one of a man who offers tokens of loyalty, sincerity, and devotion to a lady. He moreover risks his life and fortune at war and in other ventures to prove his manliness to her, sometimes for years on end. The lady bears no such burden. The preceding dialogue suggests the man's ordeals are amply rewarded by the lady's approval alone. Without context, one gets the impression of a mere woman cult, a trivial enterprise of self-abasement based on gender. But several additional factors need to be considered. First, courtly love developed in the context of a large surplus of men in Muslim Spain, and continuous immigration mostly of men, starting from the 8th century. An ongoing lack of women, and the chivalric culture that resulted, eventually came clashing with the misogynic culture of the lower social classes further north:

> In northern France, more than anywhere else in Europe, the clergy as well as the bourgeoisie of the 12th and 13th centuries, indulged in a rough and unbridled antifeminism, and even among the minor country nobles the doctrines of chivalry and the corresponding poetry had scarcely any success. By contrast, the greater nobles, ambitious knights, and self-conscious courtiers were intent on distinguishing themselves from the rest of the population and adopted from the south the new style of personality cultivation.
>
> — Herbert Moller, *The Social Causation of the Courtly Love Complex*

In addition to men being more numerous, the gentlemen who bid for love were of a lower social status than the ladies they courted. They may have been errant knights with commoner status looking for entry into nobility, as it was still possible at the time. Thus the fabled ennobling power of love could also mean a noblewoman could, at her discretion, confer her loftiness to a suitor of lower status, through marriage or by simple association. Among the nobles and ambitious knights, pursuing social promotion was an intense preoccupation. Eventually this upper-class behavior was emulated by the lower rungs of society. Custom came to demand men assume servile roles toward women. Instead of permeating the culture, the lofty ideal of courtly love devolved into pettiness:

> Thus it came to pass, through the overwhelming formative power of northern French culture, that a ritualized public adoration of ladies in combination with servant-like action toward them — such as granting ladies precedence, picking up their things, performing all kinds of small personal services, etc. — became a badge of social superiority for men.
>
> — Herbert Moller

Courtship became a shadow of what it once was, now amounting to mere posture:

> ... each says when he seeks to woo,
> Hands joined and kneeling,
> "Grant that I may freely serve you, lady,
> As your man." and she thus receives him;
> I rightly judge to be a traitor
> A man who says he's her equal and her servant.
>
> — Marie de Ventadour, in Rosenberg's *Songs of the troubadours and trouvères*

There is no longer any question of ennoblement here. Once a servant, always a servant. The knight asks the lady to either make him her equal, or to ask him to love her more, so that he may be her equal. Gui d'Ussel replies:

> Lady, it's a shameful opinion
> For a lady to defend
> That she will not hold as equal
> The one with whom she's made one heart of two.
> Either you'll say (and this won't flatter you)
> That the man should love the lady more faithfully,
> Or else you'll say that they're the same,
> Because the lover owes her nothing except by love.

For our times, an egalitarian approach is expedient and will no doubt foster honesty and mutual respect. Gender should not be a basis for an unequal relationship. In general, we partner with people of more or less equal socioeconomic status, so it is appropriate we give *mutual* assistance and service, and also give *each other* the abstract "reward" of love. A household could start from the raw material of ordinary humanness and become ennobled by mutual loyalty, respect, and appreciation. Beyond supporting each other, the partners could also commit themselves to the service of love, for instance by committing to nonviolence, and by practicing the virtues conducive to a deep and sincere relationship.

If you are courting someone, rather than groveling and offering unneeded favors, secretly commit yourself to the service of love. Practice the best virtues you are capable of. As you come to know each other, you will go through changes, which the other will not fail to notice. Even if the courtship fails, it will still bear fruit. You will know joy and sorrow. You will have loved to the fullest extent possible. For your efforts, painful as they may be, you will be a better lover. Such delicate pain is worth enduring.

Spontaneity and respect of the other

Spontaneity is one of the uncontested features of courtly love. This contrasts sharply with the conjugal duty sanctioned by the Church at the time.

> Go away, forced love! It is the free and very hidden love that exalts our senses: that which is taken in hiding is sweet.
>
> — Burkhard von Hohenfels, Minnesänger (1212–1242)

Respect of the other means to respect the other's choice to love us, or not. We draw on the relationship's benefits gently and sparingly. Schnell relates the story of Gautier d'Arras, disfigured in combat, who feared Galeron, the woman he just married would stay with him only out of obligation. He flees and goes into hiding in order not to impose on her. She discovers his hiding place, affirms her love for him, and asks him to return home. He accepts only after being assured of her love.

Moderation and reason

There is agreement in the courtly literature that restraint is necessary for love. If we give our emotions a free rein, we will not have the temperance we need to conduct our love affair. Instead, our random emotions and personal baggage will take over and consume the relationship.

> He who can keep Measure can boast of courtesy. He who wants to comprehend all and accumulate all that he sees, needs to reduce excess in all, or else he will never really be courteous.
>
> — Bernard de Ventadour

We need reason and discernment in order to sort through our feelings, and extract the exalted from the habitual or carnal. This helps us overcome infatuation before it takes hold of our life. We also need a kind of realism in order not to invest overmuch in one who will not love us back.

Forbearance ("disposition à la souffrance")

Longing, painful periods of separation, exhilarating reunions followed by tearful parting, uncertainty about future encounters, such is the lover's lot. Love without suffering is not real:

> Gaucelm, those who love as impostors do not feel the suffering of love, and one cannot have great value without suffering and sorrow; no one can have merit without vexation and sacrifice...
>
> — Albertet de Sisteron, troubadour (1194–1221)

Privacy and decorum

Love needs discretion and privacy to express itself properly. Any manner of gossiping and rumor-mongering must be strictly avoided, in keeping with the "golden rule" of treating others how we want them to treat us. According to the Second Law of Love, a person who cannot keep a secret can never be a lover.

The troubadours reserved their worst curses for those who took to damaging others' love relationships. They even had an Occitan word for it, *lauzengier*. The term originally meant a flatterer, and then came to also mean a false seducer, a slanderer, and a malicious gossipper who enjoys ruining other people's love affairs. What to do against the *lauzengiers*? The lover-troubadours felt powerless to counter their vile moves. It is very difficult to counter gossip, because arguing in one's defense easily becomes gossip in turn. If for example one says "so-and-so gossiped," that easily becomes fodder for more gossip, and also it looks petty to worry about one's reputation. In the end, the best solution was to trust in the good judgement of one's beloved.

How courtly love helps us

Courtly literature has developed a rich array of ideas of love abstracted from worldly constraints, such as marriage and social class. This includes the elaborate jurisprudence recorded by the courts of love.[18] But is it at all relevant to us? It is worth asking whether courtly love was really practiced (and practical), or was only a literary phenomenon.

Schnell's article provides insight into this important question. In his estimation, courtly love was not a customary practice but a literary ideal, whose value was determined by the context in which it was read, usually out loud: to inspire, to entertain, to critique common behaviors, or for the prestige of a princely court. Courtly-love literature played a role in verbalizing contemporary concerns and humanizing social conflicts: rivalries and tensions between the troubadour and his lady, between rivals, or between poets. By showing dilemmas, such as between love and marriage, the literature suggested a legalistic manner of conflict management, playful and spiritual, for the problems people experienced at the time: the tension between service and reward, the jealousy of rivals, public versus private, overwhelming emotion versus self-control. Conflicts were elevated to the status of literary discourse, a step toward nonviolent resolution.

But the troubadours, knights and ladies were not just entertaining themselves. They were keenly interested in elucidating the intricacies of love. This can be seen in their impassioned debates, and in the existence of the courts of love between the twelfth and fourteenth centuries. One can then conclude that their material was based on real situations, and real conflicts or moral dilemmas, to which they offered reasonable solutions outside of violence and normative traditions, going so far as disagreeing with the Church. By reflecting on their wisdom and trying to see their relevance to our situation, which may not be all that different, we can discover our own, principled values of love.

9. How to kiss like in the movies

The first time a couple kiss often marks a special moment in a new relationship, the beginning of a privileged rapport, and perhaps becoming lovers. In the archetypal movie kissing scene *the man*, fired up with self-assurance, gets hold of his love interest and moves to kiss *her*. She hesitates or even resists him for a brief moment, but in short order she is overcome by passion and kisses him back enthusiastically. Does it ever happen just that way? Is this movie scene relevant to our non-fictional, and possibly non-picturesque reality? Does gender have anything to do with it?

Sex educator Clarisse Thorn offers an interesting discussion about how the first kiss can come about. The vast majority of the time, *the man* is expected to initiate the first kiss. A small minority of women prefer to initiate. Some are of the opinion *the man* ought to know, intuitively and unfailingly, the exact moment during the courtship when *the woman* will be receptive. This is a genuine concern for a man and a worrisome burden. At this stage of courtship, there is very little explicit communication about the relationship, or whether there is in fact any kind of relationship. The situation is in flux, even fragile. A fast move can cause embarrassment and increase, perhaps fatally, the parties' sense of separation. But waiting too long can cause disappointment, which can also be very difficult to recover from.

Some believe the first kiss is too delicate for guesswork, and *the man* should simply ask *the woman* whether she would like to be kissed. The intuitive faction argues that asking, by verbalizing the situation, *ruins the moment* by eclipsing any spontaneity that might otherwise take place. To complicate matters, some women will even refuse to kiss a man simply because he asked, because asking is a sign of unmanly uncertainty. The explicit faction retorts such a woman does not deserve to be kissed in the first place. The intuitive faction replies that such women are so numerous that to exclude all of them would not be practical.

While the debate rages on, it seems a real work of art could take place right between the two sides of the argument. Ostensibly, the movie kiss is created by the man's bravado *and* social intelligence. The woman is just a passive consumer of his initiative. In real life, both parties have come to this point and developed feelings for each other *together*. As people become attuned to one other, they exchange little physical gestures, such as holding hands or touching each other's arm, even for brief moments. Without this small amount of physicality, it is very hard to imagine how people will come to kissing each other, let alone spontaneously. This light physical contact develops naturally over time, even from the first meeting, starting with just a little warmth and enthusiasm. Now you have a nonverbal communication channel, and are growing and showing steady affection for each other. This is not gender-based particularly.

Do not try to estimate or guess when the other wants to be kissed. Kiss him, or her, *when you feel like it.*

A reader given to pettiness will surely recoil in horror at the above sentence. What about *consent?* Do you really mean to *act on your feelings* toward a person who *might not want* to be kissed? *Unthinkable!* But this situation relies on people having become attuned to one another and as a result there is a low likelihood of disconnect. In any case, the solution to the problem of consent is trivial, and offered by *Mystery* (Erik von Markovik), a pickup artist who teaches men to attract and seduce women. In the so-called 90/10 rule, you approach the other 90 percent of the way, and the other must advance the remaining ten percent. If the person who does not initiate the kiss must travel ten percent of the way to meet the other, then consent is obtained implicitly and wordlessly. Beyond the need for consent, this "90/10 rule" encourages mutual investment, but that does not matter. Relax, and enjoy a thrilling and romantic kiss.

10. Lovemaking: a preliminary exercise

In Part One we have explored karezza, and we also have touched on the notion of our sexual energy as a basis for the entire body's vitality. Our body is wholesome and complete. Our lovemaking does not need to be ruled by reproductive urges. Here is a preparatory exercise you can perform on your own. It will make you more aware of your sexual energy and prepare your body for a more subtle and sustained exchange with your partner. This is a simplified synthesis of different Chinese, Indian, and Tibetan traditional systems. This exercise and its variants are known as *vajroli mudra*, *sahajroli mudra*, the microcosmic orbit, the inner flute, etc.[19]

Find a quiet, private place to practice. You may do this exercise standing, lying down, or preferably sitting on a chair. You need to locate the pubococcygeus (PC) muscle. It is located in the pelvis and connects the tailbone to the pubic bone. It is responsible for stopping the flow of urine, so the simplest way to locate it is to hold your legs spread apart and contract it as if to stop peeing. Breathe at a normal to slow pace and slightly deeper than usual. As you breathe in, contract the PC muscle. As you breathe out, relax.

As you continue this breathing, contracting and relaxing pattern, visualize some energy or warmth going from the area just below your navel[20] downward to energize your genitals. Bring the energy down as you breathe out. As you breathe in, visualize the energy going from the genitals to the tailbone, up the spine and into the brain. Touch the tongue to the roof of your mouth as a switch to enable the flow of energy from the forehead down the neck and to the front of the body. As you breathe out, bring that energy down the front of your body to the genitals and back up to the navel area, completing a circle.

Perform this practice by linking breathing, PC contraction and relaxation, and visualizing energy going up the spine and down the front of your body. Optionally, accompany the above with slight pelvic movements, thus:

- Breathe in; contract the PC muscle. The energy goes up the spine; the tailbone tilts toward the back.
- Breathe out; relax the PC muscle. The energy goes down the front of the body; the tailbone goes forward.

The ascending energy is *yang* in nature, and feels electric. The descending energy is *yin* in nature, heals the internal organs, and feels like a nourishing fluid. The interplay of yin and yang is at the heart of the traditional Chinese worldview. Here it concerns the inner workings of the body, some of which are compared in the table below:

Yang	Yin
Immaterial	Material
Produces energy	Produces form
Generates	Grows
Non-substantial	Substantial
Energy	Matter
Expansion	Contraction
Rising	Descending
Above	Below
Fiery	Watery
Function	Structure
Excitement	Inhibition

PETTINESS

The ancient Chinese also say women belong to yin and men belong to yang, but that does not help our pettiness problem. In fact, the more we experience the balance of yin and yang in our body, and the more we see our body, male or female, as made up of the interplay of polar opposites. This way, we come to an experiential understanding of the similarity of men and women. We all have both the masculine and the feminine in us, however defined. From that standpoint, the human body is mostly hermaphroditic, and homosexuality is nothing special.

During conventional sex, arousal causes pressure to build up in the genital area. Energy builds up until it can no longer be held and is expended as orgasm, with ejaculation in men. This exercise offers a way to recirculate the accumulated energy up the spine, rather than expending it. Not only is this beneficial to one's health, this approach can also help men delay ejaculation for as long as they want, after a few weeks or months of practice. A man also gains some degree of control over his reproduction. (This is one of the least effective methods of birth control.) By handling sexual energy this way, both men and women can discover an alternative to orgasm-centered sex, and a subtler, longer lasting, and more satisfying approach to lovemaking.

This exercise as presented is generally considered safe. However, it is important to keep a light touch and not be forceful or build up energy deliberately. In *Opening the Energy Gates of Your Body*, Taoist educator Bruce Kumar Frantzis warns: "There are deeper, more secretive and esoteric aspects of this practice, however, that must be learned under the strict guidance of a teacher to prevent bodily harm." The point is circulation, not buildup. In particular, if you suffer from hypertension, it is not safe to accumulate energy in the brain. At the end of the practice session, it is safest to direct the energy all the way down to the soles of your feet. Otherwise, you normally end the exercise by letting any accumulated energy rest in the navel area.

11. Gracious love: the bouncy snow lion

As we begin to live in ethical, caring, and compassionate ways, our lives become touched by a joyful grace. Such a state of grace is called *perkiness* in the Shambhala warrior tradition. It is symbolized by the mythical white snow lion with a turquoise mane who roams the mountains, enjoying the crisp and fragrant air of the lofty peaks.

> The snow lion is vibrant, energetic, and also youthful. He roams the highlands where the atmosphere is clear and the air is fresh... Just as the snow lion enjoys the refreshing air, the warrior of perky is constantly disciplined and continuously enjoys discipline. For him, discipline is not a demand but a pleasure... This warrior is always aware and never confused as to what to accept and what to reject.
>
> — Chögyam Trungpa, *Shambhala: The Sacred Path of the Warrior*

The discipline of the perky warrior is to extract greatness and cheerfulness from the raw material of the human condition. By training through reflection, contemplation, and bravery, you come to a sharp view of what is elevated and what is ignominious.

Contemplations

Just as in Part One, as part of a meditation session take one of the topics below and reflect on it for a few minutes. Let the questions challenge you for a moment, and reflect on any emotion this evokes. Finally let go of all thought or feeling and end with a few more minutes of meditation.

> *Imagine a society where people, on the main, are content with their sexuality, and men and women live in harmony with each other. This is no utopia; such places do exist.*
>
> *Did it ever make me truly happy to win an argument?*
>
> *Envision a perfectly gender-egalitarian society. Does it seem incongruous to you?*
>
> *Is it possible for a society's gender-role division to harm both sexes? If so, why and how does such a role division persist?*
>
> *How much of me is male? How much of me is female?*
>
> *How open is my heart right now?*
>
> *Imagine seeing your spouse or partner, or someone whom you desire very much, in another's arms. Practice being at peace with that. Beyond being at peace, wish them to be happy together.*

Some people may find this last contemplation exceedingly hard. It is absolutely important to practice it diligently, even if only a little bit at a time. Sexual jealousy is almost certainly the keystone of the entire edifice of pettiness. For the sake of grace, overcoming jealousy is well worth the discomfort.

Part Three
Vanity and Charm

Vanity and Charm

> The sight of a feather in a peacock's tail, whenever I gaze at it, makes me sick!
>
> — Charles Darwin (1860)

12. What is attractiveness?

The conventional meaning of vanity is to elaborate on oneself, as for example by adorning the body, or to use the analogy of the peacock, displaying an exuberant personality. For the needs of this discussion, vanity is defined as our fixation on having a sexually attractive partner. The notion of attractiveness, and whether attractiveness even exists, need to be considered. We then reflect why desiring an attractive partner, which again seems so *natural and instinctual*, is in fact another serious problem we must overcome to free up a more authentic expression of love.

It would be expedient and politically correct to say sexual attraction is a matter of personal taste, our inalienable freedom to choose our partner. In a petty society, where a good deal of subtle or overt coercion may be present, reaching for the freedom to choose our partner is reasonable. However, beyond the concern about freedom, our criteria for a desirable sexual partner are worth examining. What do women want? What do men want? If we ask one another, we may simply get convenient platitudes for answers. A scientific inquiry yields insightful and less pleasant results. David Buss, the professor of psychology cited previously, coordinated a very large survey of men's and women's sexual preferences in thirty-seven cultures. Men value physical attractiveness (an indicator of health, fertility, and reproductive value) in women, and prefer women who are younger than themselves. Women on the other hand value earning potential, ambition, and industriousness in men, and prefer men who are older than themselves. The most striking aspect of these results is the consistency of most of the attributes men and women find attractive in each other, across many cultures, rural or urban, rich or poor, modern or traditional.

Concerning men's desire for physically attractive women, Naomi Wolf argues in *The Beauty Myth* that standards of female beauty are arbitrary and promoted by television, magazines, and other media. Indeed the insistence on the part of both men and women on a physically attractive partner has increased dramatically with the advent of modern communications, while men's stronger insistence on physical appearance (as compared with women's preferences in men) has remained a constant.

But the attributes men see as attractive in women are, with few exceptions, remarkably unchanging across cultures as well as over time within a given culture. David Buss gives us the recipe for male standards of female beauty as "full lips, clear skin, smooth skin, clear eyes, lustrous hair, and good muscle tone... a bouncy, youthful gait, an animated facial expression, and a high energy level," as shaped by millions of years of evolution. To the above list one should add the ideal female waist-to-hip ratio, which in the United States has consistently remained at 0.7 over several decades, even as the ideal amount of body fat *varied* over the same time. Women with a waist-to-hip ratio different than 0.7 are seen as less attractive.[21]

Competition

In any given society, there is remarkable consensus about who is sexually attractive, and therefore who is not. We may ask why any of this might be a problem for finding love. To simplify for the sake of argument, the rich could mate with the beautiful, and the plain-looking could pair up with the less moneyed. In this benign hierarchy of attractiveness, there would be someone for everyone. We may know men's and women's preferences, but we have yet to examine how insistent we all are on getting our wish.

In one study, the professor of psychology Douglas T. Kenrick and collaborators asked 93 undergraduate men and women what their minimum criteria would be for various stages of involvement with the opposite sex, from a single date to marriage. Those surveyed were explained the meaning of percentiles, e.g. someone in the 70th percentile of kindness is kinder than 70% of others, but less so than 30%. Almost universally, selectiveness increased for an increased level of involvement, i.e. more was required for marriage than for a single date. Women indicated the minimum acceptable earning capacity for a man to be eligible for marriage is the 68th percentile. That is to say, women on average find two thirds of men unfit for marriage on account of their earning capacity alone. Fewer than a third of men are seen as husband material, and even fewer if more criteria are added. As for men's desire for women's physical attractiveness, a woman must look better (presumably according to the criteria above) than 61% of other women in order to be seen as wife material. Only 39% of women meet those criteria, and again fewer if more criteria are added. Both men and women on average also require than someone be kinder than 71% of their peers, and more intelligent than 65%, to be found suitable for marriage.[22]

Let us ponder this for a moment: the men and women surveyed probably were of average looks, earning capacity, kindness, and intelligence.

> Please accept my resignation. I don't want to belong to any club that will accept me as a member.
>
> — Groucho Marx

This excessive selectiveness may be the single greatest cause of scarcity and frustration in love: We all want *someone special*. But if we all put value in the *same criteria* of attractiveness, it simply isn't possible for all of us to be special in the same way. If someone is willing to consider us as a potential partner, we will in all likelihood see them as not good enough for a simple reason: wanting us, they probably belong to a lower attractiveness percentile than we do. If someone sees us as special, they likely are not special to us. This alone is a formidable obstacle to any sexual encounter, be it meaningful or not.

This is not lost on Mystery, who points out quite pragmatically that by his approaching alone, a man will inform a woman that her "value" is greater than his, thus ensuring rejection. This is not only about men approaching women. In a speed-dating experiment where men and women would take turns being the approaching party, researchers Eli Finkel and Paul Eastwick found that the tactical advantage accrues to the person being approached, regardless of gender.

Not only is this percentile bias a great obstacle to sexual encounters, it also causes all sorts of direct and indirect pressures to live up to unrealistic norms of attractiveness. Pressures women experience over their appearance has been well documented by Naomi Wolf and others. Women feel not pretty enough, starve themselves to become thin, undergo various cosmetic surgeries, spend small fortunes on beauty products of dubious value, go on punishing exercise regimens, feel guilty about not doing enough to enhance their appearance, etc.

Men are under no less pressure, but over things other than their physical appearance. One would think that women prefer men with money and a high social status because of their historical relative lack of power and money. This is known as the *structural powerlessness hypothesis*. This hypothesis does not stand up to a simple test:

> Interview studies of both medical students and leaders in the women's movement reveal that women's *sexual tastes become more, rather than less, discriminatory as their wealth, power, and social status increases*. Fifteen feminist leaders, when asked what they sought in a man, recurrently used words that connote high status: "very rich" or "brilliant" or "genius." Lavish dinners, large tips, stunning suits, and so forth were regularly referred to. In short, these high-power women wanted super-powerful men.
>
> — Jerome Barkow et al., *The Evolution of Sexual Attraction*

13. The problem of the peacock

Darwin's original idea of evolution concerned the adaptation of species to survive in their environment. He did not at first make sense of the peacock's feathers. Not only does this elaborate and colorful plumage not offer any discernible advantage toward survival, it actually makes the poor bird much less able to fly. If survival were all that mattered, how could evolution allow such extravagance? Darwin coined the term *sexual selection* to describe the evolutionary effect of the peahen's preference for colorful peacocks. The birds with more colorful and abundant tail feathers have more mating opportunities, and therefore peacocks have evolved large and colorful tail feathers. Such a preference may have had at one time the value of selecting for healthier or stronger birds. Over time the preference simply came to stand on its own, to the detriment of flight, which would better allow the peacock to escape predators. Thus an increased chance at reproduction comes at the cost of a reduced ability to survive.

One could still argue this is all lively and good. Competition promotes beauty, luxury, and continuous improvement. By definition, this is beyond the need for survival and is a measure of prosperity. The capitalist system allows for such luxuries, and the law of supply and demand regulates the market. This is true if we accept we are commodities that can be ranked and graded by percentile according to narrow criteria, and then discarded when we become less desirable. These criteria of desirability may be meaningful or meaningless to us.

> *Everyone* is disposable. So maybe you feel like men judge you for your looks. Maybe you feel like men can ditch you at any time for another pretty girl. But men, we contend with being judged for our wealth. There's always a richer guy. Gold-diggers make men disposable.
>
> — Cited by Clarisse Thorn

> When a girl becomes marriageable her parents should dress her smartly, and should place her where she can be easily seen by all. Every afternoon, having dressed and decorated her in a becoming manner, they should send her with her female companions to sports, sacrifices, and marriage ceremonies, and thus show her to advantage in society, because she is a kind of merchandise.
>
> — *Kāma Sūtra*

Imagine the large numbers of men competing with one another to be part of the acceptable 32% top earners, and moreover spending a good deal of their hard-earned money in superfluous displays of social status, such as expensive outings, cars, and clothes. Because of this pressure, modern society has developed wealth and conspicuous consumption[23] far beyond our reasonable needs, in a way that now causes environmental degradation, natural-resource depletion, and destabilizing social inequities.

Not only does this fixation on attractiveness make it hard (in fact, theoretically impossible) for couples to form, it can also go on poisoning relationships long after they are established. The men and women who do not belong in the upper percentiles of attractiveness have to settle for less than what they want, on account both of their choosiness and of that of their prospects. The disproportionate representation of highly attractive women in the media causes men to feel less satisfied with, and less committed to their long-time partners.[24] And as we just saw, many women also tend to judge their own bodies as inadequate. Likewise in marriages where husbands earn less than their wives, the divorce rate is twice as high as in marriages where husbands earn more. When husbands earn less, they tend to despise themselves, and wives tend to despise their husbands too.[25] In summary, male and female criteria of attractiveness are adhered to and enforced by both sexes. And the obvious downside of the valuation of sexual attractiveness is the experience of not being attractive:

> Growing up, I was overweight and never popular with the boys. They either ignored me or called me names like "fatso" and "tub o' lard." My own brothers were among the name-callers, and my father didn't seem to want anything to do with me. I figured I was disgusting to all males because of my body.
>
> In high school and college I managed to find three boys who would date me. One was gay. The other two just wanted to use me for their own pleasure and convinced me that this was as good as I would ever get.
>
> — Anonymous[26]

It is generally considered shallow to judge a woman by her physical appearance, yet appearance plays a large part in men's mating decisions. This habit is not the result of contemporary shallowness, it is deeply embedded in the human experience, independently of culture. Likewise women readily admit to being attracted to dominant men, men of large means, and men of high social status, oblivious to competition over dominance and resources being a major cause of inequality, social instability, and even war.

> An example I often use to illustrate the reality of vanity, is this: look at the peacock; it's beautiful if you look at it from the front. But if you look at it from behind, you discover the truth. Whoever gives in to such self-absorbed vanity has huge misery hiding inside them.
>
> — Pope Francis (2013)

Such male and female criteria of attractiveness do not indicate a person's real worth, spiritual or moral. They are just entrenched old habits. They are not even an indication whether such an attractive person would satisfy us in a casual sexual encounter, except for the appetite we ourselves bring to the encounter. In other words, to want sex with someone because of his or her attractiveness may not be shallow, but it is purely self-referential, self centered. Wanting long-term relations with another person based on his or her conventional attractiveness alone is to forgo the opportunity to apply more relevant criteria toward a fulfilling union and meaningful procreation. Instead, we just breed prettier peacock feathers, and also a good deal of competitiveness and aggression into our own culture. It is said, "Why pollute the source from which we all drink?" Doing so represents a passive, consumer mentality, a waste of resources, and a complete lack of contribution toward a vibrant and meaningful culture. It is truly a gigantic missed opportunity.

Self-esteem

We could easily call such hierarchical ranking of attractiveness the *law of percentiles*. If we belong to a high percentile, we feel good about ourselves. If we do not, we feel we are a lesser human being. Self-esteem is essentially related to our self-perceived "mate value," which includes not only physical attractiveness but social dominance as well.[27]

Women are attracted to men who display confidence, because that is a sign of social dominance. Men shun women whom they see as lacking in beauty on the pretext that they have *low self-esteem*. Yet to deem someone unattractive amounts to visiting a subtle amount of violence on that person. We place them on a lower percentile than we think we belong to, thereby contributing to the lowering of the other's self-esteem. It is quite circular. Even if ranking the attractiveness of others were meaningful, it would not be fair, because we tend to overrate ourselves by desiring a partner of a higher percentile than ours. This makes for a society preoccupied with meaningless imperfections in its members, and whose collective self-esteem sinks constantly in generalized, mutual devaluation. The only things left to make up for this lack of self-respect are consumerism and vapid displays of male and female sex appeal, for all to see.

Obsession

We may at one time meet a person as a lover, or only as a prospect who, *if only* we had more of him or her, would *make our life perfect*. Only this does not happen, and we never seem to get enough of that person. *If only… nothing else will do.* This approach is fatally flawed: having such heightened interest, we lose all sense of proportion, appear excessively needy, and are therefore unattractive to the other. Having our wish is not possible in such conditions. We are at a dead end.

It seems that something similar was going on with our courtly knights and dames. If a knight would pursue a lady for many years, performing heroic deeds to impress her, in the faint hope of gaining the tiniest morsel of approval, surely a sentiment akin to obsession must have been at play. No other experience would have been compelling enough to sustain a lengthy romantic pursuit with such long odds. Beyond the obvious literary effect, concrete results must have been quite faint. Moller remarks that the combination of an imbalance of the sex ratio, social ambition, and "the dread of losing status" probably explains the "semi-realistic features of troubadour poetry." Thus "many of the poets voiced disappointment and even disgust with the meager results of their efforts."

In order to overcome obsession, we first need to see the reality of the other person, and not just be blinded by our desperate wish. We might genuinely appreciate the other person's goodness and may even have plenty to offer him or her. Only this relationship is doomed, and therefore exists only in our mind. The desired person is not, and never will be, interested in our mental vagaries. We may think we are discerning some reciprocal interest, but it is not wise to rely on such biased intuition. By recognizing our state of obsession as nothing more than a figment of our imagination, and moreover by realizing that life before meeting this person was not so bad, we can find the strength to let it go. It is by far the sanest way.

14. Approaches to overcoming vanity

The law of percentiles can be defined thus: we want a partner of a higher percentile of conventional attractiveness than we belong to. To summarize, vanity is insubstantial, self-centered, competitive, predictable, and circular. While it seems to be very much a norm of human behavior, it is also illogical and disadvantageous. We all think we are going to beat vanity at its own game, and we all end up trying to outcompete each other over the same criteria of attraction. Instead of being ourselves, humble and content, we puff ourselves up, because we want someone more attractive than ourselves, according to percentile rankings. Of course, this aspect of vanity is not operative all the time. If it were, it would be completely impossible for couples to form. Human relationships come about in spite of vanity rather than because of it. There must therefore be a principle that goes against vanity. One might call it *charm*, because such a principle would be powerful, compelling enough, to bring about a good-enough sexual union in spite of our self-defeating tendency to hold out for more.

For all its faults, vanity is not shallow. It is almost immovably embedded within us all. The pervasiveness of vanity suggests that if any solution has ever been found, it has been found in obscurity, or in incomplete form. Let us look at some of the approaches people have taken to deal with vanity.

The principled artist's approach

If we had a very long time, we could simply do nothing and wait it out. Conscious of our inherent worth as human beings, we could simply refuse to add anything to it, just as adding one more ingredient can ruin a perfect dish. Being human is good enough. We face the same problem as many great artists and writers, who refuse to debase their craft to sell more.

Likewise the idea of being a worthy, good human being merely from the fact of being human, and of letting our *inner beauty* shine through is in theory possible. Only if society is overwhelmingly given to mass commercialization and mass sex appeal, it may be a very long time, perhaps even decades, until our heroism finds an outlet. A great artist or writer could become famous only long after he or she is dead. This may be acceptable, because the point of great art or literature is to leave a lasting and inspiring legacy. If we are looking for love, it may not be practical to wait that long. All along, we will be tempted to play the game of attractiveness, even as we dislike it and dislike ourselves playing it.

The pickup artist's approach

Modern pickup artists are men who train their personalities to have just the kind of charisma that women delight in and find sexually attractive. Moreover, they wield an armamentarium of strategies and tactics designed to overcome a woman's perception of her own attractiveness versus that of the pickup artist. It can be argued this is dishonest and harmful, because it seems to undermine another person's self-esteem. It does not have to be. Such an uncanny skill set plays with the vanities of both men and women in a dynamic exchange of views. In many cases, men turn to pickup methods because they see no alternative. A man may be decent and worthy, but only needs to be a bit shy or weak in social skills to not be attractive to women. This is how Neil Strauss, a pickup-artist friend of Mystery, describes his past predicament as a young man:

Vanity

> I spent my teens and most of my twenties lonely, desperate, and woefully inexperienced, sitting mutely on the sidelines while women obsessed over guys whose appeal boggled me.

Reading pickup literature can give us valuable insight into human nature. Just like the peahen's preference evolved in concert with the peacock's plumage, pickup techniques show the vanities of men and of women as intimately linked. Let us examine a typical pickup routine, as explained by Mystery. We do not need to understand every move and every bit of jargon to see, in graphic form, the material the pickup artist is working with. As we just saw, the law of percentiles puts the one approaching the other at an automatic disadvantage, regardless of gender. What ensues is a tactical play of the parties' respective self-valuations, until the scales are tipped back to a stable, equal state. The graph below illustrates the dynamics of the initial exchange:

1. At first, the woman is not approaching anyone, but is about to be approached by the pickup artist. She has the situational advantage, as any man who approaches her is at a disadvantage.
2. But the pickup artist is confident, well-dressed, not needy, etc. He stands out and is slightly intriguing.
3. The pickup artist goes on "demonstrating value" and is appreciated by other women in the group, while he "negs" his target. ("Negging" in pick-up jargon means teasing a woman both to reduce her situational advantage and to stand out from other men by showing he is not a flatterer who craves her attention.)
4. The woman, seeing his "value," now tries to gain his approval, a situation he is more than willing to

exploit. The tables are fully turned. The woman struggles to win the man's attention!

5. Finally, a more congenial rapport is established, both parties have expressed mutual interest and investment, and it is time to move to a more isolated environment for further "escalation."

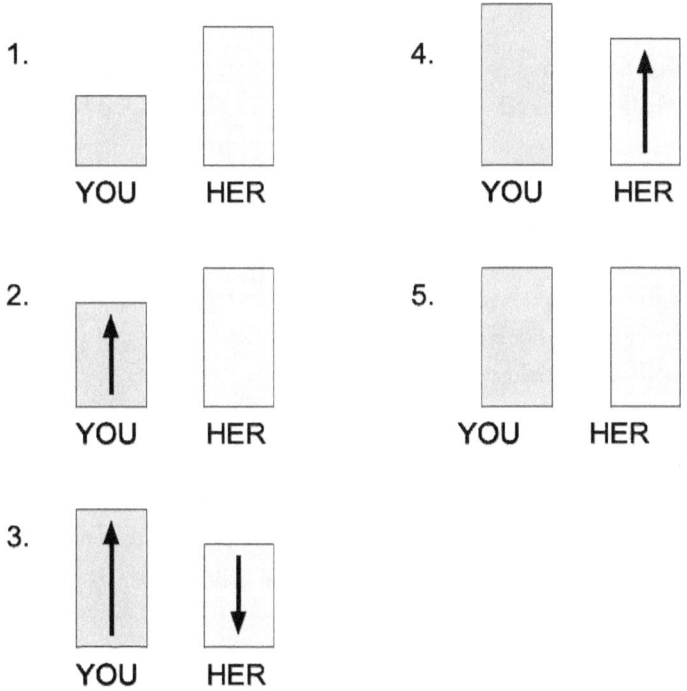

If the strategy succeeds, then the protagonists find themselves in a situation conducive to a deeper rapport. They may eventually engage in sexual relations, for good or bad. If they are good and sincere relations, there is nothing more to say. If not, the parties have only their respective vanities to blame. By examining the reality-tested insights of pickup artists, we can therefore discover how predictable we all are.

VANITY

The troubadour's solution

The proponents of courtly love were of course experienced with the problem of vanity, which confuses love with social promotion. Having an attractive mate means social success. The knight or troubadour was hopelessly dependent upon his lady's approval:

> Here the hopes, strivings, and insecurities of contemporary realities evoked images connected with deeper, more elementary needs of proving oneself worthy of being loved and being singled out for a special share of approval... What would have been painful to discuss as personal problems, could be worked through in a communal fantasy centering on the image of a woman who was able to grant acceptance in privileged society, self-assurance, and a feeling of personal worth in a world of changing values.
>
> — Herbert Moller

The impassioned knight may not know whether he is smitten by love, or merely tantalized by the prospect of ascending the social ladder. He asks the lady to be a little easier, in effect to get past her own vanity, that he may gain her favor:

> Lady, heed not rank and riches in your treatment of me, but your honor, for you can change it from good to better; and the profit will be mine, the glory yours. He who exalts the exalted does not do very much; but he who exalts and upholds the humble gains thereby the favor of God and friends and fair renown.
>
> — Aimeric de Peguilhan, troubadour (1170–1230)

Only his bidding is doomed, because he is addressing a woman of higher social rank, and moreover asks her to make the effort of considering him anyway. The abstract rewards that he suggests she will gain in return, are not even his to give. It will not work to ask another to curtail his or her own vanity. There is no merit or effort on our part. From the other person's standpoint, this is even suspect. We must overcome our own vanity. Marcabru (1130–1150), a troubadour of humble birth, found happiness just that way. Instead of looking for a promotion, He mingled with "women of the people":

> I might better spend the time with women of the people. Wherever I go there are many of them, and I find the one who wants me. She is my heart's delight. What good is too high a goal?

15. The *ahal* of the Tuareg

One way or another, dealing with vanity means contending with the law of percentiles. This involves not only ourselves but the entire mating marketplace. A change of culture is needed as a stable and durable solution. We may not change all of society at once, but we may be able to cultivate a circle of friends or salon, much like the medieval courts of love. The courts of love were looking for a humanistic approach beyond the normative, religious, and materialistic ideas of the time. As we saw, courtly love suggested concrete solutions to the problem of pettiness. We now turn to a more dynamic circle of men and women, the *ahal* of the Tuareg of North Africa. While the European court of love was rather like a tribunal or a salon composed mostly or only of noblewomen, the ahal is an assembly of men and women intent on finding love with one another, rather than just discussing it.

The Tuareg are a nomadic, matriarchal tribe living in the Sahara desert. They are nominally Muslim, but also hold many animistic beliefs. Their unique characteristic is that adult men veil their faces as a matter of decorum and personal dignity; women do not. The Tuareg are matriarchal in that the women own most of the property, including their dwellings, and hold an important place in society. The transmission of property and of many aspects of the culture, including writing, music, and the art of love, is matrilineal. Unlike their Arab neighbors, unattached women enjoy unfettered sexual freedom. The foundational mythology of the Tuareg traces them to Queen Tin Hinan, who lived in the 4th century. However, the ahal is probably much older and may go back to the Nasamones of Libya in the 5th century BCE or even earlier. *Ahal* means a meeting, a conversation, or an interview. It has been called a musical gathering, a poetic meeting, a court of love, a love school, and an encounter. It is all of those.

People dress in their best clothes to attend the ahal. Some men have been known to travel long distances, even hundreds of kilometers, to attend. All adults are welcome if they are unattached. Married and older women also sometimes attend if they want to contribute to the propagation of the Tuareg culture of love, without looking for a mate. It is a rather formal gathering, presided over by a queen of the ahal elected for the occasion. She ensures the appropriate decorum and the transmission of correct values.

When all are gathered, the women elect *soltana*, or queen, and sometimes a *soltan*, or king, but never a *soltan* alone. Their role is to enforce the custom of the *ahal*, usually by imposing humorous forfeits on those who do not behave.

> And then there are the innocent games… A man must know how to answer questions correctly. For instance, he may be asked, "Whom do you love most, this woman or that one?" Were he to answer one or the other, he would be jeered, and incur a punishment, or have to pay a forfeit. The woman preferred would be ridiculed by her companions, because one must not manifest any overt preference, but answer, "I love them both."
>
> — Maurice Benhazera, *Six mois chez les Touareg du Ahaggar*

The ahal is also a place for verbal jousting. Here is how a young man attempts to best one rival:

> … Another goes behind her back and whispers verses in her ears. She bursts out laughing.
>
> This does not seem to please a young Tuareg, who strives to remember some embarrassing details about his rival's past: bad taste in clothing, an act of cowardice when he was younger, meanness toward some girl, bad behavior, etc. Thus he tries to discredit him in her eyes. And so verbal jousting begins. It is a veritable duel, where the worst affronts and accusations are directed against rivals.
>
> But this is done with extraordinary chivalry, because no fracas or argument must take place: the accused counters with much grace, and it is rare that this leads to grudges. That is the rule of the ahal.
>
> If a contender does not manage to respond with dignity, and if he resorts to rude language to defend himself

against his rival, he is excluded from the ahal, if the president so decides.

— Douchan Gersi, *La dernière grande aventure des Touareg*

In another example, one who made an impertinent remark was sentenced by the soltan to kiss the soltana's sandal, while praising her with a poem of his composition. As he seemed only half-hearted in his delivery, he was ordered to renew his performance in good faith, on penalty of further punishment.

Jealousy is frowned upon, except in the case of flagrant adultery. Sometimes husbands even tolerate their wives discreetly seeing former lovers from their ahal days.

> Gallantry, or *asri*, is *de rigueur*, and jealousy severely proscribed. Moreover, this last sentiment is unknown among the Tuareg, and if one were to show it, he would be jeered and everyone would mock him.
>
> — Benhazera

Asri here stands for keeping gallant company, although it literally means "running unbridled," in other words every manner of sexual license. It is a very broad term used to describe the status of young people from puberty, when they begin to attend the ahal, and generally of any unmarried person. Virginity is not valued and has no significance among the Tuareg.

> In fact, women are easy, more or less. Some give themselves to anyone. Some grant their favors only to a small group of friends, but to grant them only to one would be judged as very bad taste and as a sign of perversion.
>
> — Henri Lhote, *Les Touaregs du Hoggar*

When a man desires relations with a woman, he places his hand in hers, palm up, and asks, "Are there any tidings?" If she accepts his offer, she says, "there are many." When she wants to refuse, she says "not too many" or any discouraging formula, or even pretends to be asleep. When the ahal is over, couples who have made contact in this manner meet again privately under the starry desert sky or in the woman's tent.

Much like the courtly songs of medieval Europe, the poetry sung or recited at the ahal deals almost exclusively in love and war: the grace and elegance of women, the heroic deeds of men, the fire of passion, and the overwhelming pain of love. Note the etiquette of not favoring only one woman:

> I tell my dromedary: walk and do not fall asleep!
> I want to be, this very evening,
> with the women with ivory complexions.
> And now I stagger, lost in love.
> My heart is consumed, nothing but an empty wineskin.
> God help me confess that.
> I love Tinirt [the *soltana*], but I love all her [female] neighbors too!
>
> — Cited by Émile Steinilber-Oberlin

Some aspects of the ahal help manage pettiness (for example, frowning on jealousy). The ahal also reduces vanity to some extent, through its dislike of excessively selective men and women: if facilitates actually finding a partner, thus defying the law of percentiles and the devaluing of one another. On the other hand, the valuation of men's warlike qualities lacks a vision of peace, and makes men's attractiveness conditional upon a conventional and competitive criterion:

> Banditry, in the form of raiding rival encampments was, as we said, a very prominent activity with the Tuareg... it is an atavistic taste with the Tuareg, that led them to this kind of expedition; it brought together, for the circumstance, the most disparate individuals, all animated by the same spirit of adventure and pillage, and was reinforced by the consideration it enjoyed among women. On that count, one can say that more than one looting raid was motivated by nothing other than the desire to please them, and especially to bring them beautiful clothing and jewelry taken from others. The vanity of men blended with that of women in perfect manner.
>
> — Lhote

We see here an example of a matriarchal society which, far from being peaceful, actually incited men to violent raiding, while the women stood as the beneficiaries. Inevitably, some men would be seen as more virile than others on the basis of their violent actions. Therefore, it can be said that even with the ahal as a civilizing influence, the vanities of men and women have not subsided in Tuareg society.

This being said, the colonial powers of the early 20th century ended the culture of raids and counter-raids. Gone are the days of heroic songs of deed and the noble Tuareg women's love as a reward for chivalrous merit. For inspiration, the ahal has to make do with trivial events, such as retrieving a stolen donkey, even as the thieves went unpunished. As of Steinilber-Oberlin's writing (1934) the ahal is just an archaism.

Regardless, the ahal could still be a forum for the deliberate propagation of a culture of love. Its members receive, through song and poetry, and also by exposure to each other, the transmission of their cherished values.

A circle of friends

The nomadic lifestyle of the Tuareg, who are very poor to begin with, is threatened by global warming impoverishing an already very arid desert, forced sedentariness, and regional warfare. The tradition of the ahal has nearly vanished into an obscurity as dark as its origins.[28] It may be up to us modern people to recreate its glorious institution. We do not have to copy the ahal exactly, because we do not have the same values. For instance, the Tuareg have a rigid, race-based caste system, which at one time amounted to a form of slavery.[29] We do not need to cultivate warlike or other competitive values either. But we can still be inspired by the ahal's form and methods. Such a forum could help manage sexual jealousy, and pettiness in general, encourage decorum, and foster the more positive and universal values of courtesy and gentleness in love. We could use the same time-tested methods of song, poetry, verbal jousting, guessing games, and other cultural means. It is not hard to imagine how such a circle could be formed. Some ground rules are necessary to ensure participants feel safe, as they may not know each other at first. A more or less equal number of men and women is needed, and some accommodation should be made for persons with same-sex orientation. People would be encouraged to make cultural contributions, such as poems or music. Since this is a place where people come to find love (and also to offer it), people should dress their best, as when going on an important date. Desired values can be cultivated by having a person teach (but only a little), or facilitate the event. This cannot be too hierarchical, as for example always having the same organizer, because the participants' full expression is needed. Spontaneity is needed to help people get a sense of each other. Thus a kind of courtship takes place: each can speak to the group, affirming values, sharing experiences, but without being forced to do so — free expression can also mean being silent. This way, the group takes on a life of its own, rather than being moored in dogma or just one person's ideas. An environment conducive to love can then develop, even if society is not perfect.

16. The peacock redeemed

There may no be ordinary means of overcoming vanity completely, and if so we will therefore be vexed by it continually. One way or the other, we may end up swallowing our pride, because vanity does not offer a happy ending. We will be disappointed as we see our or our partner's body decline with age. To invest in the body is to invest into a decaying asset, an unwise investment.

> When 900 years old you reach, look as good
> you will not, mmh?
>
> — Yoda in *Star Wars, Episode V: The Empire Strikes Back*

Likewise we will be disappointed when we see that the manly traits of social dominance and bravado promise much, and offer little, toward lasting happiness. We will feel deceived when we realize our partner's display of attractiveness did not deliver what we expected. It would be a mistake to blame each other. The best thing to do is assume responsibility for our useless and predictable criteria. Why not take the lead and anticipate this ghastly situation?

Now our problematic peacock is also an old Indian symbol. He is said to eat snakes and scorpions, and from that makes his colorful plumage. This stands for the transmutation of negative experiences into the nectar of wisdom. Likewise, we can develop a taste for going against the grain of our base instincts of attraction. Suppose we now develop meaningful relations with someone whom we might have considered a reject, or defective goods. Going against that instinct feels like eating poison, at least at the beginning. The point is not to pursue an unattractive person on purpose, but rather to ignore the idea of attractiveness altogether, a bold move. Instead, we rely on our own sense of what is worthy and good, our very own, heartfelt values. As the other person's good qualities become prevalent, the preoccupation over attractiveness recedes. No competition takes place. In fact we no longer see competitive people as competition at all, because they are mired in vanity. This vantage point is liberating and empowering. We obtain one important benefit at the cost of bearing what in retrospect amounts to a very insubstantial frustration. We transmute the poison of vanity by renouncing our high or low or middling self-esteem. This self-esteem is nothing but a kind of currency, which we gain or lose through our successful or less successful romantic ventures, and as our attractiveness changes with age and circumstance.[30] In exchange, we obtain a deeper kind of confidence, which does not depend on anything. We have unconditional confidence, because of what the Shambhala teachings call our *basic goodness*, the sense of being fundamentally worthy no matter our circumstances.

VANITY

To rely on basic goodness is an act of courage. We trust we are fundamentally good, for the mere fact of being human. There is no need for any striving or self-appraisal. Goodness is always there, whatever we do, whether we see it or not. Even if we face problems, we can be confident we are in a workable, worthwhile situation.

Garuda's breath

As part of a meditation session, imagine a person whom you desire, an extraordinarily attractive person, right in front of you. Ideally this would be a real person in your life, whom you actually want very much. Think how wonderful it would be if this person also wanted you. Then imagine this person is rejecting you, and how wretched you feel as a result. As you breathe in, feel the elation of being accepted by this attractive person. As you breathe out, feel the misery of being rejected and unloved. Alternate feeling elated and dejected as your breath goes in and out. (Although this practice superficially resembles the practice of tonglen described in Part Two, it is not related.) As you keep switching between the two opposite emotions, begin to see their insubstantiality. As you practice, the hope of being accepted and the fear of being rejected begin to loosen their grip. Experience a larger part of your mind, which is not taken by these extremes, beyond hope and fear.

The prince and the beggar

This practice is a variant of the above. Imagine someone whom you love with all your heart as a prince or princess being paraded in full regalia in front of a crowd. He or she may be riding on horseback, or sitting on a horse-drawn carriage or in an open-top limousine, triumphant. Now imagine you are a beggar, dressed in poor clothes, standing in the crowd at the front. He or she knows you well and is aware of you, but is not paying you any attention. This beautiful person is so exalted, and you are so insignificant! Feel the contrast for a moment.

If the practice ended here, it would only be an exercise of self-inflicted misery. There is more. For a moment, consider that both of you and all those in attendance possess the same good, human heart, basic goodness, which is everyone's birthright. Even though everything suggests one person is much better than the other, it is only situational. Imagine the two of you being of equal worth. Practice switching roles back and forth: see yourself as the beggar, and then see yourself as the princely, exalted person, while the other is the beggar. Never forget both possess the same basic goodness. After some time, dissolve the whole scene by imagining it turning into a billow of confetti of different colors, until it is completely gone. Experience the empty space for a moment.

17. The outrageous charm of the garuda

Relying on our inherent basic goodness, rather than on our conventional attractiveness, we can afford to defy the mating market, and even treat it with disdain:

> You, the richest person on Earth,
> who have been going around begging for a living,
> stop being the destitute child.
> Come back and claim your heritage.
>
> — Thích Nhất Hạnh

VANITY

> You carry a basket of fresh bread on your head,
> Yet you search from house to house for crusts.
> Knock inside yourself, no other door!
>
> — Rumi, *Masnavī 5*

It is a splendid proposition, unheard of, yet tantalizingly within reach. It is the charm we have been looking for, the power to overcome vanity. In the Shambhala tradition, this is known as outrageousness, a state beyond any competitive or comparative logic, beyond hope and fear:

> When you hope for something in your life, if it doesn't happen, you are disappointed or upset. If it does happen, then you become elated and excited. You are constantly riding a roller coaster up and down... Outrageousness is symbolized by the garuda, a legendary Tibetan bird who is traditionally referred to as the king of birds. The garuda hatches full-grown from its egg and soars into outer space, expanding and stretching its wings, beyond any limits. Likewise, having overcome hope and fear, the warrior of outrageous develops a sense of great freedom... The analogy for this is a good, self-existing sword — desire to sharpen it will make it dull. If you try to apply a competitive or comparative logic to the experience of vast mind, by trying to measure how much space you have fathomed, how much is left to fathom, or how much someone else has fathomed, you are just dulling your sword...
>
> The warrior of outrageous also possesses great mercy for others. Because you have no obstacles to expanding your vision, you have immense capacity of working for others.
>
> — Chögyam Trungpa, *Shambhala: The Sacred Path of the Warrior*

Having overcome violence, we possess great gentleness. After overcoming pettiness, we have grace. As a further extension of the drive toward greater humanity, we become powerful, *charming*. Yet there is no desire to exploit that power, because this charm is made of gentleness and goodness. It does not depend on any achievement, or outdoing our competitors. It is self-existing charm, relaxed, fresh, and candid. We now come to realize we had it all along. It is therefore symbolized by a mythical bird who hatches full-grown from its egg. The more we relax, the more charming we become. On the contrary, if we try to manufacture charm, we end up puffing ourselves up and become vain all over again: we dull our sword. Isn't that extraordinary!

Instead of connecting with others because of attractiveness and vanity, we relate on the basis of our shared humanity. It is a magical situation, the power that comes from trusting our basic goodness.

If we stop measuring or comparing ourselves, our partner, or our experiences, we come to the realization that we hold the immense power of procreation, the power of life — and also the power of death, through refraining. Having cultivated kindness and nobility of spirit for a long time, we want to impart life rather than death, and this generosity allows our charm to emerge. There is no threat or competition at all. This power is obtained not through aggrandizing ourselves, but by relaxing deeply, and being fully confident in the power of basic goodness, which does not depend on anything. The vainglory of the materialistic world now seems so inefficient and insignificant. Outwardly, we may not have any material advantage to show. But inside, we are full of richness and power, soft, and humble.

As with the mythological peacock who uses poison as food, vanity is the fuel of this realization, a stepping stone, almost a pretext. Nothing is happening other than our basic goodness, always present. One analogy sometimes used is that of the sun, always present but sometimes obscured by clouds.

18. What's all this tantric stuff, anyhow?

In recent years, there has developed an interest in so-called tantric sexuality, and circles have formed around activities designated as such. Tantra is an ancient and venerable Indian spiritual tradition, of which there are many strands, including many Buddhist, Jain, and Hindu lineages. The syncretic Baul religion, which unites Vaishnavite, Sufi, and Buddhist strands, is tantric too. In its many traditional forms, tantra is a catch-all phrase for a vast set of practices performed with the intent of reaching enlightenment. In those various traditions, enacted or imagined intercourse often plays a part. But the goal is enlightenment, not sex. Yet in modern, Western presentations of tantra (and perhaps in its place of origin also), there has been much distortion, commercialization, and sensationalism, to the point that it is hard to discern any remaining trace of an authentic spiritual tradition:

> The paucity of research and publications on the Tantric heritage of Hinduism has in recent years made room for a whole crop of ill-informed popular books on what I have called "Neo-Tantrism." Their reductionism is so extreme that a true initiate would barely recognize the Tantric

heritage in these writings. The most common distortion is to present Tantra Yoga as a mere discipline of ritualized or sacred sex. In the popular mind, Tantra has become equivalent to sex. Nothing could be farther from the truth!... Their main error is to confuse Tantric bliss (*ānanda, mahāsukha*) with ordinary orgasmic pleasure... they are sadly misleading, for instead of awakening a person's impulse to attain enlightenment for the benefit of beings, they tend to foster narcissism, self-delusion, and false hopes.

— Georg Feuerstein in *Tantra: The Path of Ecstasy*

To have any chance of avoiding self-delusion, we should at the very least know what we are trying to accomplish. If we want sex or a relationship, we should pursue that, and if we want enlightenment, we should pursue that. To state without proof that one leads to the other, or that one subsumes the other, is courting a dangerous illusion. In either case, in order to avoid narcissism, we need to dedicate this pursuit to a goal higher than our own fulfillment, such as living out a vision of an enlightened society, or universal love. Cultivating gentleness, grace, and charm can be a stepping stone toward realizing such a vision, because that entails a selfless attitude.

A definition of tantra

Tantra has been defined as a spiritual practice which uses mantra recitation, visualization, devotion to a living guru, etc. But many disciplines involve these elements without being tantric. Mantras are used in many contexts. For example the *prajñāpāramitā* mantra appears in a *mahāyāna* Buddhist *sūtra*. The vedas of Hinduism also have mantras. By definition, neither vedas nor sūtras are tantra. Visualization, including the above exercises, is not tantric as such. Devotion to a guru is a fixture of Indian society in many disciplines that require mentorship, such as music. The definition of the *vajrayāna* or tantric path as *path of the goal*, used by several schools of Tibetan Buddhism may be helpful:

> ... here we are talking about the sudden path, the direct or sudden path of tantra. This is the realization that does not depend on a progressive, external buildup or unmasking. It is realization eating out from the inside rather than unmasking taking place from the outside... The approach here is to regard oneself as being a buddha already. Buddha is the path rather than the goal.
>
> — Chögyam Trungpa, *Crazy Wisdom*

Regardless of the definition we choose to rely on,[31] the proper transmission of tantra ultimately depends on receiving its teachings from an undistorted lineage. Herein lies the problem: no historical, authentic tantric tradition actually focuses on sex for its own sake. Needless to say, if there is no such tradition, there is no point in pretending otherwise.

The goal of tantra

One particular teacher (Osho in *Tantra Spirituality & Sex*) cites from the *Vijñāna Bhairava Tantra* as a basis for giving extensive teachings on sacred sex. However, a reading of the *Vijñāna Bhairava Tantra*, along with commentaries by serious proponents of this tradition such as Daniel Odier or Jaideva Singh reveals a classic Hindu text of the Kashmiri *Shaiva* tradition. A small part of the text mentions the possibility of a spiritual experience through sex. On the main, the purpose of the *Vijñāna Bhairava Tantra* is to realize union with the divine through a variety of means, which depend upon individual practitioners' capacities and inclinations. Sex is only one of many methods. Yet it seems most so-called tantric sex has been drawn from this particular textual tradition. Other texts, some of which have been identified by Miranda Shaw in *Passionate Enlightenment*, would seem more appropriate, as they have greater emphasis and detailed instructions on sexual practice proper, while the *Vijñāna Bhairava Tantra* treats sex as only a little more than a metaphor. In any case, all the above purport to bring about enlightenment. This goal has nothing to do with the pursuit of pleasure, which may even be an obstacle:

> First, one must meet with a suitable partner who has the esoteric empowerment... so that at the time of intercourse when passionate attachment and the concepts associated with it arise, this is experienced as the creative energy of pristine awareness... If one does not know this, it is just attachment.
>
> — Padmasambhava

The "esoteric empowerment" above is absolutely required of both partners who are attempting such traditional practices which, again (and again) have enlightenment as their goal, and require much preparation. This ensures we have trained with a qualified teacher, with the correct motivation and sufficient discipline, almost always over a very long period of time. Receiving of the empowerment acknowledges we are ripe for whatever practice we receive, from a teacher who knows us well. Pursuing exotic practices with pleasure as the main goal, and all the more without empowerment, results in the opposite of spiritual liberation, which is "just attachment."

Some go so far as to describe the *Kāma Sūtra* as a tantric text. The *Kāma Sūtra* is simply an ancient manual of conduct for the upper classes of India. It offers advice on courtship and marriage, as appropriate for the society for which it was written. It has become famous in the West for its candid descriptions of intercourse. None of this makes the *Kāma Sūtra* tantric by any definition.

Rather than debasing a venerable tradition, it would be better to be honest about what we are looking for. We can then make the best of whatever means are available to help us achieve that goal. If we want ordinary sex, we should pursue that and call it a day. If we want to learn seduction for good or bad, pickup literature and workshops are on offer. If we want enlightenment, or a rich spiritual life, we may be better off with mainstream spiritual teachings, which do not treat sex or relationships *per se*.

Having said that, we may still want a spiritual approach to love and sex, and somehow intuit something magnificent is at stake. We have come so far, conquering formidable enemies. Could we at least experience a glimpse of the ultimate? If such a possibility exists, would that be tantric?

The divine within

If we want a profound experience of intimacy, and somehow foresee some ecstatic experience to be had, going back to the definition of tantrism as the "path of the goal" may offer us some guidance. We have the divine in us; we are enlightened already, or possess *basic goodness*, but often fail to experience it in our day-to-day life. Rather than being uniquely tantric, the idea of *inherent enlightenment*, or the *divine within*, is widespread. We may at times forget his idea has been part of many spiritual and religious traditions, as these attest:

> When you seek God, seek Him in your heart — He is not in Jerusalem, nor in Mecca, nor in the hajj.
> — Yunus Emre, Turkish poet and Sufi mystic (1238–1320)

> Man starts not from a premise of original sin, but from the divine spark of equilibrium in the soul which enters the flesh at birth from the world of the gods. To act in foolish anger or petty selfishness is to depart from this original gift of interiorized nobility and conscience.
> — Robert Farris Thompson on the culture of West Africa

> Heaven and earth cannot contain me, but the heart of my faithful servant contains me.
> — Hadith Qudsi

> All power is within you. You can do anything and everything. Believe in that. Do not believe that you are weak; do not believe that you are half-crazy lunatics, as most of us do nowadays... Stand up and express the divinity within you.
> — *The Complete Works of Swami Vivekananda*

> No one has ever seen God; but if we love one another, God lives in us and his love is made complete in us... And so we know and rely on the love God has for us. God is love. Whoever lives in love lives in God, and God in them.
> — 1 John 4:12 and 4:16

> The coming of the kingdom of God is not something that can be observed, nor will people say, "Here it is," or "There it is," because the kingdom of God is in your midst.
> — Luke 17:20–21

VANITY

> The Hawaiians are gentle natured people living in deep spirituality with the land. Their gentleness is reinforced by the communal life on an island. Their spirituality is strengthened by the land and other elements of nature. The prayers and chants of the Hawaiians acknowledge the divine spirits within all people and the things around them.
> — Paige and Gilliatt

If we stop measuring or comparing ourselves, our partner, or our experiences, we come to the realization that we hold the immense power of procreation, the power of life; and conversely the power of death, through refraining. Having cultivated kindness and nobility of spirit for a long time, we want to impart life rather than death, and this generosity allows our charm to emerge. There is no threat or competition at all. This power is obtained not through aggrandizing ourselves, but by relaxing deeply, and being fully confident in the power of basic goodness, which does not depend on anything. The vainglory of the materialistic world now seems so inefficient and insignificant. Outwardly, we may not have any material advantage to show. But inside, we are full of richness and power, soft, and humble.

> The average man is so crisp and so confident
> That I ought to be miserable
> Going on and on like the sea,
> Drifting nowhere.
> All these people are making their mark in the world,
> While I, pig-headed, awkward,
> Different from the rest,
> Am only a glorious infant still nursing at the breast.
>
> — Tao Te Ching 20

As with the peacock who uses poison as his food, vanity is the fuel of this realization, a stepping stone, almost a pretext. If there is no real teacher of tantra, it is best just to experience such realization as it happens, without trying to make it happen. Nothing is happening other than our basic goodness, always present. One analogy sometimes used is that of the sun, always present but sometimes obscured by clouds.

19. How to make love

Books describe sexual poses and techniques in endless detail. These methods, including so-called tantric ones, can be applied with or without feeling. What does that have to do with our inner world? How do we share our inner experience meaningfully? This cannot be any less important than physical acts. For the suggestions in this chapter, there is a need for balance between saying too little, which is inconsequential, and prescribing too much, turning an otherwise spontaneous act into an unfamiliar nuisance. What follows is a suggestion as to how your lovemaking can embody sacredness. Practice whatever feels comfortable and meaningful in your situation.

At the appointed time, mark a clear boundary between the world of day-to-day activity (which is often rife with small and large conflicts), and the space reserved for lovemaking. To that effect, you can use props, such as soft or rich clothing, special lighting, or incense. Their purpose is not living out an exotic fantasy, or even a sensual one. The point is to create a safe environment to meet one another in your most basic state: free of worry, fantasy, neurotic projection, emotional neediness, or any kind of hurry. You are creating a space made up of gentleness and grace, so that you can be yourselves. You are reaffirming your commitment to no longer rely on any amount of violence or pettiness. Also leave behind concerns of conventional attractiveness, and thus abandon vanity. You do not need to beautify yourselves. You are not in the process of selecting each other. At that moment, you are faced with one another free of mundane distractions. There is no more struggle or worry of any kind.

If you want, bow to each other in the Añjali Mudrā (palms joined before the heart) and say *namaste*. This traditional greeting, widespread throughout Asia in different forms, means "I salute the divine in you," while also acknowledging your own. Although this form of greeting can also be a gesture of reverence and respect, you are greeting yourself and your partner simultaneously. Again, the point is not to produce any exotic effect, but to acknowledge the divine or enlightened quality in yourselves. This experience is independent of any particular religious or spiritual tradition, and is no doubt also available to agnostics and atheists.

A state of ambiguity, even a mild panic, ensues. You are mingling your presence with that of another person. Having abandoned the vanity you are accustomed to, an inchoate, barely formulated thought arises. *Is this person right for me?* Before it can even be entertained, the thought is lost in a torrent of sensation. Staying with the uncertainty has the delightful taste of fearlessness, or stepping outside of the limitations you have made for yourself. You feel soft and vulnerable toward the other, yet uncommonly bold. This is what overcoming vanity and the law of percentiles feels like.

You may even feel some mild regret at ever having thought of rejecting your partner. You can now show tenderness in simple physical gestures, which escalate quite naturally and lead to foreplay as we know it.

For intercourse, simply combine karezza and the microcosmic orbit described previously. Karezza lays the ground with the idea that sex does not need to be driven by reproductive instincts. The microcosmic orbit shows that you do not depend on a partner to balance you or complete you. You are complete and powerful as you are. You are meeting one another because you want to, not because you need to. Make a faint sound while breathing, allowing yourselves to synchronize your breaths as well as any bodily movements.

Do not rush.

Up to this point, no tantric technique has been performed by our definition. You have only laid the ground to allow the experience of divinity within, divinity meeting itself through the interplay of two actors. Union is not created, it is inherent. It has already occurred, as if mixing water with water. You do not need to join anything with anything else. You are recollecting a primordial, blissful state. You just give yourself to the flow of experience. Every sparkling sensation, seemingly caused by the interplay of male and female energies, or yin and yang, is a manifestation of divinity or enlightenment. Gender does not exist at this level.

> Penetrating the place where heaven and earth have not divided and yin and yang do not reach, directness will attain success… the true self is the self that is prior to the division of heaven and earth, before your parents

conceived and gave birth. This self is the self that is in all animate things, birds and beasts, grasses and trees. This is what is called buddha-nature.

— Takuan Sōhō, cited by Thomas F. Cleary

Enjoy movement, stillness, and physical poses as you see fit. None of this really matters, save for the view of divinity, or inherent enlightenment. This experience could rightly be called tantric. There is no technique; you are just open to it.

Only focusing on physical pleasure or even emotional fulfillment, or pondering your partner's attractiveness (or lack thereof), is losing the view of divinity. Pursuing pleasure or a comfortable mental state is just ordinary sex. Even closing your eyes to better enjoy the experience entails a risk of falling back on the ordinary pursuit of pleasure. If at any moment you feel you or your partner are losing the inspired view, use an agreed-upon method, such as making eye contact, or saying *namaste,* as a reminder. Consider this practice does not make you anything special. Thinking you are special would just be vanity, because all beings have basic goodness. Think of it instead as a communion with a larger world.

This kind of lovemaking, not being a pursuit of conventional orgasm, does not end with any particular event. You can make it long or short, deep or symbolic, intense or relaxed, according to what suits you. Only don't overdo it:

> Just as you should not eat until you're stuffed, so you should not make love until you're exhausted. You should slightly desire food after a meal, and you should still desire your lover after you've lain with her… Sometimes

less is more. Don't satiate your sexual desire, or it will turn into distaste.

— Mantak Chia, *Taoist Secrets of Love*

Gently end the session with another bow to each other. You can now engage your world again, energized by lovemaking.

Contemplations

As in Parts One and Two, as part of a meditation session take one of the topics below and reflect on it for a few minutes. Let the questions challenge you for a moment, and reflect on any emotion this evokes. Finally let go of all thought and feeling, and then end with a few more minutes of meditation.

I am very attractive. How do men and women relate to me? How do I relate to them?

I am not attractive. How do men and women relate to me? How do I relate to them?

How do I relate to attractive persons of both sexes, as opposed to the way I relate to non-attractive ones?

What are my peacock feathers? (In other words, Which traits or attributes do I have, that have null or negative survival and moral value, but which others find sexually attractive?) *Which of those do I maintain or cultivate deliberately? At what cost?*

Envision a society that knows no discrimination on the basis of sexual attractiveness.

Will I still love my partner when he or she is no longer attractive?

Remember a time when you were happy for no particular reason.

Part Four
Agenda and Mystery

Agenda and Mystery

Love is the master astrologer,
It gazes into the mysteries.
There may be explanations, but silence is better.
The pen became a writer,
Yet it broke when it wished to write about Love.
If you wish to explain Love,
Take your intellect and throw it in the mud,
For intellect offers no profit in the business of Love.

— Rumi, *Masnavi 1*

20. The last great enemy

Having come so far in our journey, we probably experienced great joy and great relief, as well as hurt and disappointment. We see and understand more about the behaviors of men and women, including our own. We are not a prisoner of our habitual tendencies, because we can easily identify them as one kind of enemy or another, and remedy them. Our perception is now much more refined. Of the four great enemies of love, we can say violence is the most obvious; pettiness is the most prevalent, by being normative; and vanity is the most intractable, because it is embedded, and embeds us, in the world of commerce. The fourth enemy, our *reproductive agenda*, is the most insidious. It is present in so many situations that we do not suspect its existence at all. It is hiding in plain sight, like the air around us.

From violence to vanity, we have proceeded from the grossest to the subtlest of obstacles. Where does the journey stop? Does it go on with subtler and subtler refinements, like an endless martial art with an indefinite number of belts of different colors? The pinnacle of the spiritual experience is above the preoccupation of achieving further and further stages of development. Here is how Chögyam Trungpa expressed the idea in his celebrated *Sādhanā of Mahāmudrā*, a liturgy often recited at the meditation centers he established in the West:

> The kingdom of no-dharma, free from concepts,
> Is discovered within the heart.
> Here there is no hierarchy of different stages
> And the mind returns to its naked state.

There comes a point where a surfeit of sophistication brings diminishing returns, a kind of vanity or decadence. Making a profession of the spiritual life betrays the spontaneity and ineffability of love. If we make a project of spirituality, we may become clever or encyclopedic. We may even con the world into believing we are experts on love. But we will not have the immediacy to enjoy anything. Worse yet, instead of opening our heart and extending ourselves to others, we may end up using our spirituality to build the fortress of ego:

> Ego is able to convert everything to its own use, even spirituality... When we have learned all the tricks and answers of the spiritual game, we automatically try to imitate spirituality, since real involvement would require the complete elimination of ego, and actually the last thing we want to do is to give up the ego completely. Ego translates everything in terms of its own state of health, its own inherent qualities... At last it has created a tangible accomplishment, a confirmation of its own individuality.
>
> — Chögyam Trungpa, *Cutting Through Spiritual Materialism*

"The complete elimination of ego" means surrendering and truly opening up. There is no love without surrender. Rumi made this point again and again:

> Die in this love, die right now
>   that when you die in this love
>   you will become more alive...
> Die in this love, in front of the beautiful king
>   That when you die, you will become a king and a queen.
>
> — Rumi, *Divān-e Shams*

> Love is not in morals, knowledge, or books.
> Whatever the discourse, that is not the path of lovers.
>
> — Rumi, F 395[32]

In order to do that, we must be free of any mental scheme or overlay that would get in the way. The last obstacle comes about when, having lost the old habits of violence, pettiness, and vanity, we begin to feel an existential void in their place. It is as if we were missing our old neuroses, which had been our lifelong companions. According to the Buddhist tradition, fear of space is our worst fear, the fear we do not exist:

> Q: Why do you think that people are so protective of their egos? Why is it so hard to let go of one's ego?
>
> A: People are afraid of the emptiness of space, or the absence of company, the absence of a shadow... It is generally a fear of space, a fear that we will not be able to anchor ourselves to any solid ground, that we will lose our identity as a fixed and solid and definite thing. This could be very threatening.
>
> — Chögyam Trungpa, *Cutting Through Spiritual Materialism*

When relating to love and intimacy, this is what happens: If we have violence in us, we experience empty space as a literal threat to our existence, and we confuse the fear of not reproducing with the fear of dying. We try to allay that fear by asserting ourselves at any cost; for example, we become arrogant. If we are petty, we feel space threatens us by a lack of moral certainty, and by emotional blankness. We fill the space by making or following rules, and by rationalizing our instinctual emotions, such as our sexual jealousy. We may even recruit our religion in the service of pettiness. If we give in to vanity, vastness makes us feel insignificant, and we try to make ourselves important by seeking out an attractive partner.

Past these obstacles, our reproductive instincts do not disappear, but they become more refined. We still feel the same existential void, only now we want to fill it with people, with ideas, and with activities. We want to perpetuate ourselves, and in this way to escape the terrifying void of existence. Stripped of familiar neuroses, we feel raw and vulnerable. It is unbearable, and we want to fill the emptiness with a sex partner, intimacy, a family, children, or whatever we can find. Our reproductive drives, up to and including our precious *sexual orientation*, are an escape from reality. What reality? That of our own mortality, no less.

To see how familiar this dilemma is, ask yourself: which do I want, love or sex? Love or marriage? Which is the means, and which is the end? Which one will I sacrifice for the other? Which is more important, love or the other thing?

Unconditional love

That we have such a choice at all is fascinating. Obviously, our ancestors have not always made love a priority. If they had, we would not be around. Love is rare, while sex and marriage occur in industrial amounts. Not all the things we could want are *just things*. Sex, marriage, and family require many conditions to happen in a good way. Real love is elusive, unconditional, and incredibly spacious.

> The warrior, fundamentally, is someone who is not afraid of space. The coward lives in constant terror of space... Cowardice is turning the unconditional into a situation of fear by inventing reference points, or conditions, of all kinds. But for the warrior, unconditionality does not have to be conditioned or limited.
>
> — Chögyam Trungpa, *Shambhala: The Sacred Path of the Warrior*

On the surface, we can understand unconditional love as loving someone even as they become old or sick or poor. Beyond those criteria, if love is truly unconditional, it also does not depend on the passage of time, so that there is neither *falling in love* nor *falling out of love*, as with the infatuation described previously. Such love is not created, and is therefore unending as well.

It is a state which no specific condition or set of conditions brings about, except for our being available to it. All we can do is recognize love, if and when relating with another person makes recognition relevant. On the other hand if we pursue sex, or family, or any similar goal, that will eclipse the unconditional. Such pursuits, once again, are often seen as legitimate, natural, or even *highly moral*, as for instance in traditional Chinese culture:

> The Chinese believe that their lives are continued in the lives of their children and that, so long as generation succeeds generation, the predecessors are perpetuated. The maintenance of the family continuity is one's greatest responsibility to one's ancestors, for failure to produce

offspring means not only the end of the family line but the death of all the ancestors as well. Mencius has said: "There are three things that are unfilial, and to have no children is the greatest of these." The illiterate farmers may not be familiar with the literature, but they are fully aware of their duty in keeping the family tree alive.

— Martin Yang, *A Chinese Village*

Moral as this duty may be, it does not provide any space for the immediacy and freedom of unconditional love. We will be too busy looking for a partner, maintaining a marriage, and raising children, to pay attention to much anything else.

21. Everyone's agenda

Since unconditional love cannot be brought about by conditions, what is left for us to do? We can recognize our reproductive agenda is an obstacle, and then step beyond that. For figuring out what the components of our agenda may be, let us examine what could make love conditional rather than unconditional.

Seduction

The courtly knights and dames of medieval Europe knew of spontaneous love versus forced love. But the spontaneity we are talking about here is more than individualistic sexual freedom. Unconditional love is free of causes and conditions, so it cannot be made to happen. It is spontaneous. If we use our charm to try and fabricate it, we are simply trying to force our will on another person. We need to renounce seduction, power games, and in fact every manner of control, so that love can come and touch us. The meditation teacher Susan Piver relates in *The Wisdom of a Broken Heart* a time when two readers asked her what kind of love to pursue. She answered that we cannot strategize about love, much as we would like to. We can only welcome it when it manifests and mourn its loss when it is gone. The only thing we can do that will make any difference is to keep our hearts "tender, soft, and alive, no matter what." She describes that effort as "the only battle that matters."

Attachment to an outcome

Even if we do not try to seduce another, we may still hold preconceived ideas of love, and hope situations will turn out in a certain way. If for example someone whom we love becomes our partner, love is seen as triumphing, and if not, we call the love unrequited. In our ordinary perception, the latter amounts to failure. If a dating relationship leads to marriage, that is judged as success; if not, one partner or the other may see the relationship as *not going anywhere*, or even a *waste of time*, and desert it. This kind of love is not unconditional, it is qualified.

The beautiful wedding

Look at the guests at your wedding. They all look *so happy*. They say, congratulations! But when pressed, people readily admit that being married is no guarantee of happiness. Marriage can be good or bad; there is no way to tell in advance. If the outcome is unpredictable, why are the guests happy? *Best wishes* is all they are able to say. No one will tell you that you are rolling the dice, and certainly not your *loving parents*: they already are asking for grandchildren.

This systemic ignorance is the telltale sign of a ubiquitous agenda of reproduction, and not of love and happiness. Confusing love with sex or marriage is a bias we inherited, evolution's slick handiwork. Evolution is no divine being. There is no one to care whether you are happy. This veil of confusion lingers over generations simply because it produces more babies.

Sexual magic

A peculiar form of attachment to an outcome is sexual magic. It consists, more or less, in formulating a particular wish during intercourse. This is intended to produce certain results, as Osho disciple Margot Anand explains:

> Sexual magic... has the power to fulfill all kinds of desires, including:
> - Personal healing and transformation
> - New love relationships
> - Greater intimacy and harmony in existing relationships
> - Material manifestations such as financial abundance, a new home, or a new job.

Paschal B. Randolph was an American occultist and physician in the 19th century. He presented a detailed and complex system of magic that became influential at the time, which he claimed could achieve all sorts of worldly and spiritual goals, and ultimately solve all social problems, ushering a ideal new world, utopia.

Randolph's system seems to be the basis of many modern practices of sex magic. The concern here is not whether such magical practice brings about the desired effect or not, or even whether such power could be used for nefarious purposes. The point is that using sex for such concrete aims makes us lose sight of its much greater potential, the expression of love. Love does not want to be made to serve an egoistic agenda.

One could argue some of the goals, such as "personal healing and transformation, new love relationships, and greater intimacy and harmony in existing relationships" are spiritual goals, and we could safely attempt to attract them through such practice. This leaves us with a subtle problem: we can have a materialistic, and therefore egoistic attitude, even when pursuing ostensibly spiritual goals.

> Self-deception is a constant problem as we progress along a spiritual path. Ego is always trying to achieve spirituality. It is rather like wanting to witness your own funeral.
>
> — Chögyam Trungpa, *Cutting Through Spiritual Materialism*

> "Is it right for us to pay taxes to Caesar or not?"… "Show me a denarius. Whose image and inscription are on it?" "Caesar's," they replied. He said to them, "Then give back to Caesar what is Caesar's, and to God what is God's."
>
> — Luke 20–22:25

The above sermon from Jesus tells us just that. Give your heart of hearts to the truly exalted, not to material or concrete goals, no matter how laudable. Randolph, of mixed English and African ancestry, hoped his magic would help bring about racial equality. With due respect for his aspiration, social activism is the more appropriate avenue.

> The soul and the body have separate burdens
> and need separate attention.
> For if you bind a burden on Jesus,
> You leave the donkey in the pasture.
> Do not make the body do what the soul can,
> And do not place a heavy burden on the soul
> which the body can carry easily.
>
> — Rumi, *Masnavi 5*

For those things that belong on the mundane or material plane, deal with them in their own terms. If you want a car or a house or a career, don't pray or copulate, hoping for a miracle. Go earn it instead — and make sure you pay your taxes! Do not debase your spiritual energy for material ends, even lofty ones. Save it for the spiritual journey instead; save lovemaking for real love.

For reasons long forgotten, we are ensnared by the sorcerous spell of the great enemies of love. We do not need to become like them.

> Enough, don't do magic anymore.
> First see how caught up you are in magic and sorcery.
>
> — Rumi, F 2859[33]

Becoming a guru

If we have been navigating the obstacles of violence, pettiness, and vanity for a while, we may think we finally have got all the answers. Thus, we may be tempted to indulge in an elaborate seduction game, *becoming a guru*, by seducing would-be apprentices:

You may be hoping that you will be invited to more little clubs and gatherings by your protégés or friends, who are impressed with you. The point is that you have to give up any such possibility; otherwise, you could become an egomaniac. In other words, it is too early for you to collect disciples.

— Chögyam Trungpa, *Training the Mind*

The above quote is noteworthy for its lack of qualifiers. Chögyam Trungpa exhorted his students to renounce the idea of becoming gurus. Some of them no doubt were already advanced meditators when he gave this advice. Some actually went on to become teachers in their own right. He did not say to only a few of them, *unless you are at such-and-such a stage in your practice, do not become a guru*. But he said to *all* of them: *it is too early for you to collect disciples*. Spiritual teachers cannot be self-starters or improvisers. Rumi concurs:

Since you are not a prophet, be on the path walked by the prophets.
Do not become the captain of a ship caught in a storm...
Be an ear; be quiet as a mountain.
If I speak, interpret, don't give your own opinion.
If you speak, be needy for explanations.

— *Masnavi 3*

For our discussion, there are two kinds of self-styled gurus, the general and the special. The general guru purports to teach spirituality in general, and uses that position of power to exploit students sexually and in other ways.[34] The special guru teaches specifically about love, sex, or "tantra" for financial gain or self-aggrandizement.

False teachers of life use flowery words
And start nonsense.

— Tao Te Ching 38

This is not meant to say that all spiritual teachers are charlatans unworthy of having students or disciples. But to prevent harm and loss, we need to scrutinize a candidate teacher for motivation and competence. As a rule, charlatans are far more numerous than authentic spiritual teachers, and it has been so since time immemorial. Scrutinizing a potential teacher is necessary and takes time. Where does his or her claimed knowledge come from? What lineage? How much money is involved? Is there a hidden agenda? Are students in that organization worshipping a personality, or are they engaged in proper spiritual practice? Such questions are perfectly legitimate. And if those questions are met with any resistance or indignation, that is all the more suspect.

Objectification

If love could be described as a finite list of criteria, people could be paired together simply by using computer programs or specialized Internet websites. One could search for a partner by hobby, hair color, profession, or whatever. Matchmaking websites often claim to use scientific or mathematical methods to compute matches. Eli J. Finkel and collaborators reviewed some positive and negative aspects of online dating. One concern is whether dating websites are capable of predicting the success of relationships on the basis of traits knowable in advance. Another concern is the extent and manner of our choosiness when presented with many potential partners. Three major factors are associated with the quality and durability of a relationship:

- The characteristics of the partners,
- The partners's interaction, and
- The circumstances of their eventual relationship.

Of the above three factors, the first is the one most emphasized in online dating. Obviously, it is what best lends itself to computer processing. As it happens, the last two factors are by far the most important predictors of relationship success. Yet, according to the communications scientist Jeana H. Frost and her colleagues, it appears that people spend on average six times as much of their time screening each other through browsing online profiles, and in electronic communication, as they spend in real encounters. This is true of both men and women. That is, a far greater amount of time is spent evaluating a potential partner as a mere set of characteristics, or in very limited interactions, than is spent experiencing one's interaction with that person, by meeting face to face. The latter would far better indicate how the pair might get along.

> By suggesting that compatibility can be established from a relatively small bank of trait-based information about a person — whether by a matchmaker's algorithm or by the users' own glance at a profile — online dating sites may be supporting an ideology of compatibility that decades of scientific research suggests is false. That is, these sites imply, and in some instances explicitly assert, that the essential qualities of a relationship can be predicted from characteristics of the potential partners that exist before they have met. Standing in direct contrast to this suggestion is 75 years of scientific research... indicating that pre-existing personal qualities account for a very small percentage of the variance in relationship success.
>
> — Eli J. Finkel

Not only do people spend a very large amount of time theorizing what a good partner should be, their selectiveness also tends to be based on shallower criteria as the candidate pool increases in size. Objectification is usually understood as a crude form of reductionism, such as considering a man for his bank account, or a woman for her shapely curves. But even if we evaluate potential partners using sensible criteria, that may still be a subtle way to objectify others. That simply is not the way to love:

> Because one does not see that love is an activity, a power of the soul, one believes that all that is necessary is to find the right object — and that everything goes by itself afterward. This attitude can be compared to that of a man who wants to paint but who, instead of learning the art, claims that he has just to wait for the right object, and that he will paint beautifully when he finds it.
>
> — Erich Fromm, *The Art of Loving*

The problem at hand is one of conceptualizing instead of willingly experiencing the warmth, agony, and ineffability of love. Love requires openness and vulnerability. Those require effort, while choosiness and objectification are love's good-for-nothing, poor cousins.

There is another problem: the more options we have, the more mental effort we need to make a choice, and the less likely we are to choose anyone at all. This is called *choice paralysis*. Even after we have made a particular choice, there remains anxiety about having foregone other options, and in the same article Finkel says we eventually end up less committed to our chosen partner.

Futility

Another way of holding a conditioned view of love is a sense of futility. If the world is filled with violence, pettiness, and vanity, why bother? We may think we have become old and wise, and have outgrown so many things. We are above it all. We do not need to love anyone in any intimate way. To consolidate that view one can even make oneself the perfect grandparent, uncle, aunt, in-law, wise one, disgruntled spouse, whatever job is available.

Futility can also manifest as depression, if we entertain the idea that *nothing is going on*. This comes from not appreciating our life.

A modern form of futility is to see family planning as futile. It sometimes happens we neither want to be a parent nor *not* to be a parent. In one study, the men and women surveyed who felt conflicted about having a baby used birth control less consistently.[35] Even with full access to reliable and convenient birth-control methods, we hope for the best of both worlds in a sloppy way, by using birth control inconsistently.

Heartbreak

Here is the subtlest of agendas. If our love is unrequited, we experience heartbreak, which is more subtle and more compelling than the obsession discussed in Part Three. Obsession is a fixation about how life would be better by having a specific attractive person as our lover, and not letting go. Because of the law of percentiles, our excessive interest in the other person is self-defeating. We are unattractive to the other person, and there is practically no way out. For all their seduction skills, pickup artists advise simply to let go. If the masters of seduction advise letting go, who would want to argue with them?

But heartbreak is more subtle than obsession. For heartbreak to be genuine, there must be an authentic form of love beyond vanity. If we think we are heartbroken, we must first distinguish our state from obsession. We need to examine our situation and state of mind carefully. If we are merely obsessed, we just need to let go of vanity. If we are truly heartbroken, we are still attached, past our vanity, to having this person as our lover. Letting go of someone we genuinely love is harder and more painful. We need to realize heartbreak is an imperfect form of love, because of our attachment to the outcome. When caught in such a situation, it may help to reflect this way:

> This person does not want me, but is happier with this other person — or alone. What do I want most, to have this person to myself, or for him or her to choose the happier option?

If you genuinely love this person, you want what is best for him or her. Having reflected thus, embrace selflessness, let go, and rejoice in the other's happiness. Welcome the *calamitous* pain that goes with it. There is a treasure hidden in it.

> Bird of the heart, do not fly except
>   in the air of annihilation.
> Candle of the soul, do not shine except
>   in the abode of annihilation.
> May the sun of God's grace shine upon lovers.
> So that the shadow of the phoenix of self-forgetfulness
>   may fall upon all.

> Though the lover may see thousands of
>   fortunes and blessings
> Nothing appears to them except
>   the calamity of annihilation.
> Look upon me, for I have cast myself into calamity
>   from the sweetness I have seen
>   in self-annihilation.
> What would be the value of one's own life
>   or even a hundred lives
> If sacrificed for the sake of annihilation?
>
> — Rumi, *Divan-e Shams*

That is the sweetest death you could wish for your ego, so don't complain too much. Beyond heartbreak, there is a larger and richer world, that of the warrior with a broken heart, which will be discussed later.

22. The purpose of sex

At the grossest level, we associate sex and reproduction with survival, because on an evolutionary timescale, dying an early death and failing to reproduce have the same effect. Such instinctual fears predictably lack any further discrimination. Of course, simple reason is enough to understand that the pressure of reproduction is not an individual survival need. Our drives do not need to be fueled by existential fears. Such reasoned approach will greatly reduce the tendency to act rashly. As we rid our sexuality of the predictable faults of violence, pettiness, and vanity, we may still find a residue of compulsion toward sex and mating in general. We are still greatly attached to this aspect of our lives, and we may wonder why.

We say, *Sex produces babies, therefore sex exists for reproduction.* We theorize that the purpose of sex is reproduction, and that love and marriage exist simply to provide a stable and socially dignified container for that. Such belief makes for pettiness, as for instance the common argument advanced by opponents of same-sex marriage: a homosexual union cannot produce offspring. We theorize that such a deep-rooted instinct cannot be eliminated, and we are therefore stuck with sex fundamentally being a tool of reproduction. But is that really the case?

If we believe in a creator God, it is easy to say that God created sex for procreation. Beyond that, there is nothing more to say. It is a matter of faith, a philosophical dead end. On the other hand, if we believe that sexual reproduction comes from evolution, we cannot assign evolution an intent, because it is an impersonal force; but we can try to understand the evolutionary advantage of sex. No one explains it better than professor Edward O. Wilson, pioneer in sociobiology and biodiversity, prolific author, and winner of numerous awards and honors.

Wilson argues that *asexual* reproduction is actually more efficient, if multiplication is the only goal. Bacteria can split into two in as little as twenty minutes. Fungi produce very large numbers of spores; hydras grow offspring from their trunks. A sponge can multiply simply by being broken up. This is all far simpler and more efficient than the complex process of mating and fertilization. If efficiency were the only evolutionary force acting on reproduction, we might as well have evolved to reproduce asexually.

For those who argue that sex has evolved for pleasure, Wilson notes that many species reproduce sexually without experiencing pleasure, since they have not evolved nervous systems, or only very primitive ones. Sex can also be risky and costly, because of the courtship and rivalries that occur in many species, including our own.

Moreover, asexual reproduction is more selfish, in the sense that sexual reproduction requires the sharing of genes with another member of our species, at the expense of our own genes. Sex therefore does not have a straightforwardly Darwinian origin story.

The truly great advantage of sex is that it creates diversity within a species as a hedge against environmental changes. Wilson compares a hypothetical population diversified through the sexual sharing and recombining of its genes with an asexual species. The latter do not exchange genetic material and are therefore genetically homogenous. Compared with the homogenous, asexual population, the sexually-reproducing one is highly diversified. There is a far greater likelihood that at least a portion of them will survive an incoming environmental or other adaptive challenge, while the asexual species may either survive whole, or be lost entirely from the same challenge. Diversity equals adaptability and offers a far greater chance for an entire species to survive in the long term. As a result, the vast majority of eukaryotic species and a majority of all living species reproduce sexually.

We humans have evolved along the line of diversification, not faster or easier or more efficient multiplication. We thus confidently state the fourth law of our reproductive behavior, the *law of diversity*. Our sexuality fundamentally exists for diversity, not for optimized reproduction. When compared with the well-established theory of evolution, the widespread religious idea that sex exists only for reproduction makes no sense.

The law of diversity defeats the popular idea that evolution tends to favor only one kind of individual, the *fittest*. Fit for what? Sexual reproduction exists for the opposite reason, because fitness depends on the environment. As environments change, different individuals turn out to be more or less adapted. Based on ancient and fixed criteria, vanity too runs counter to the law of diversity, and is as untenable at the above religious dogma. The competitiveness of commodified sexuality does not promote true fitness, only useless, colorful peacock feathers. On the other hand, diversity enables humanity to adapt to a changing world. It is as relevant as ever.

We have diversity built into our genes, in other words the ability to accept and unite with a different, or even very different, member of our species. It is precisely this ability to accept those who are different that allows us to love unconditionally.

Going back to the traditional agenda of perpetuating the family line, its error is easy to spot: genetically, our line of ancestry is nothing special. A family's given combination of genes is fortuitous. Its chromosomes are assembled in one particular way at one generation, only to be disassembled and reassembled at the next, almost entirely at random. Because of the many possible permutations, in addition to variations and mutations, each human is statistically unique, but made up of recycled DNA codes, which all members of the village or tribe, on the main, possess in one combination or another. If we say that our particular set of genes is distinct from that of our neighbors, we attribute an identity rather similar to selfhood to an adventitious arrangement of biochemical material, which in fact does not possess such identity. Our reproductive agenda would have us believe that we are our genes, and live on through our progeny. But our genes, unique without being special, are recombined unpredictably at every generation, with the similarly fortuitous genetic encoding of another human.

Nor is computer-aided choosiness the key to finding the right partner. Since the beginning of humanity (if that could be timed in any precise way), over one hundred billion humans are estimated to have lived on Earth. If any pairings of certain kinds of people were more advantageous than others in any obvious way, such favored pairings by now would be known and understood in most and possibly all cultures. Such knowledge is not readily available, and modern cognitive methods offer no definite solution to the problem of matching. To the contrary, it seems that science is poised to finally prove the partners' matching characteristics count for very little. The law of diversity therefore suggests that we have a much greater pool of possible partners than we think, and that our habit of choosiness is just another detriment, a subtle form of vanity similar to our preoccupation with sexual attractiveness.

If we insist on the idea of sex being for reproduction, we bring our sophistication level to that of bacteria, fungi, hydras, and sponges. We are just trying to clone ourselves, and moreover we need to expend effort to pretend that we are all the same. That is not living up to life's potential. To be authentic warrior-lovers, we must use life in a way consistent with what life provides. Sexuality means diversity in a context that changes unpredictably. Embracing diversity is not just liberalism, as for example respecting alternative sexual orientations. It also means having a fluid and open mind, beyond any fixed agenda.

> My heart has opened unto every form. It is a pasture for gazelles, a cloister for Christian monks, a temple for idols, the Ka'ba of the pilgrim, the tablets of the Torah and the book of the Koran.
> My religion is Love. Wherever its caravan takes me, Love is my faith and my religion.
>
> — Ibn 'Arabī, Sufi mystic (1165–1240)

Therefore our mind can remain uncolored and unbiased, able to accommodate love however it chooses to manifest, and indeed all of life's experiences.

23. Beyond the agenda

If we hold any preconception of love, such as seeing a particular outcome as more desirable than another, we can say we are diminishing love by conceptualizing it. So the habit of conceptualizing is our enemy, because it subtly orients our mind toward fixed outcomes.

The way to despotism and corruption lies in clinging to concepts, without access to a pure realm in which hope and fear are unknown. In the realm of the cosmic mirror, clinging to concept and doubt has never been heard of, and those who have proclaimed the true goodness, the innate primordial goodness, of human beings, have always had access to this realm, in some form.

— Chögyam Trungpa, *Shambhala: The Sacred Path of the Warrior*

The state beyond our reproductive agenda one may call *mystery*. Mystery is not about coyly hiding things about ourselves; nor is it something we do not know now, but will know later. Mystery is a natural quality we possess. We all have inconceivable depth and complexity, and are never fully known, even to ourselves. Consequently love, which engages the totality of our being, is mysterious also. If we approach someone with hidden motives, that may be devious, but it is also transparently visible; quite the opposite of mystery. Love without mystery is not real love, only a clever substitute. Love cannot be fully explained, not even by mystics and prophets. But its experience is immediate and poignant.

How do we overcome this agenda? The mystery of love could not be navigated in any comprehensive way if one did not include the poetry of 13th-century Sufi mystic and lover of lovers, Jalāl al-Dīn Rūmī, already cited in many places here.

Two warrior traditions also seem relevant. One is the Shambhala tradition, where we already saw the meekness of the tiger as an image of gentle poise and strength; the perkiness of the snow lion, for grace; and the outrageousness of the garuda, for our innate charm. Surely the inscrutable dragon, the fourth emblem of Shambhala, has something to say about the quality we are looking for, mystery.

The other tradition is that of the samurai of ancient Japan, who were in no small way influenced by Zen Buddhism. The relevance of martial arts here is not combat at all. It is not even the tiresomely clichéd *battle of the sexes*, which is caused partly by pettiness, and partly by the conflicting reproductive agendas of men and women. By now this should come as no surprise. Those are described at length in two chapters of Buss's *Evolution of Desire*, "What Women Want," and "Men Want Something Else." There is no gain, no victory to be had, except perhaps peace and understanding. One does not study martial arts for overpowering anyone. The point here is an all-encompassing spontaneity, which allows a warrior to engage the world in a fluid and authentic way, free of mental fixation or scheming.

The spontaneity of the samurai happens to be the most efficient way to fight, but we are not interested in that. Rather, the pressure of actual warfare helps us discover the proper mental attitude of a warrior. Our problem is not trivial either. We experience pressure to contend with inner and outer violence, to perform assigned gender roles, to live up to lofty and demanding moral ideals, and to meet extravagant standards of male and female attractiveness. At the same time we struggle to make sense of the existential challenge posed by our reproductive drives. We are also at war with our minds, with our society, and with each other. It should be clear that more aggression and agitation are not going to help.

The exertion and valor of the great samurai of the past teach us today not only to fight and win, but also how to be in this world, authentic and without a fixed mindset. We should be grateful to those warriors, who made such great efforts and sacrifices, and were so kind to record their wisdom for us.

24. Four mysteries of love

Because of the lack of theorizing, there is no strategy. The way to love is simply to love:

> Giving implies to make the other person a giver also and they both share in the joy of what they have brought to life. In the act of giving something is born, and both persons involved are grateful... Specifically with regard to love this means: love is a power which produces love...
>
> — Erich Fromm, *The Art of Loving*

Saying just that may not seem very helpful at first. On the other hand, trying to define love more precisely may simply yield another pile of concepts, and that might create more mental clutter, more goal orientation, and more agenda. So far we have looked at what love is not: love is not violent, love is not petty, love is not vain. Now we can also add, love is not an object or an idea that can be apprehended by the mind. If there is no objectification, then there is mystery. That is how our grasping mind works when clinging to concepts or letting go of concepts. So what? Let us see where this simple idea leads to: that true love is unconditional.

Ineffability

The conventional meaning of unconditional love is to be loyal to our partner through good times and bad times, even as he or she may become (or may already be) poor, ill, not good looking, etc. Beyond loyalty, the unconditional also means something not resulting from definite causes or conditions, and therefore not fully expressible. Love cannot be defined or pinned down as a concept or as a list of concepts:

> The nature of love is inexpressible in words. It is like a dainty dish tasted by a mute person. It finds expression very rarely in some worthy soul.
>
> — Nārada Bhakti Sūtra 51–53
>
> Love never fails. But where there are prophecies, they will cease; where there are tongues, they will be stilled; where there is knowledge, it will pass away. For we know in part and we prophesy in part, but when completeness comes, what is in part disappears.
>
> — I Corinthians 13:8–10

The last quote says, love is perfection, but prophets and learned professionals (perhaps theologians) are powerless to describe it. It cannot be known intellectually in any definitive way. But where there is love, it is self-evident. Definitions, contrived and only partially true, fall away.

Elusiveness

If we look for love and do not find it, that is completely normal. It is not bad news particularly. Not finding love, we already are in direct contact with its essence, that of being beyond the grasping mind. Our lover is elusive. We do not own our lover. Expressing love is elusive too. If we talk about it too much, it loses its power. As D.H. Lawrence said in his poem The Mess of Love, the moment we declare our love, the moment it is an understood thing between lovers, that love greatly diminishes, it becomes "a cold egg."

Oneness

Ordinarily when we look for love, we really look for what meets our criteria of love. We have shrewd opinions. If this relationship does not lead to marriage, there is no love. If there is no sexual attraction *right now*, there is no love. Since love is elusive, naturally we do not find it, much less if we have demanding criteria. By relaxing our agenda for a while, we can become more appreciative of the unconditional. The unconditional is without causes, therefore it happens all the time. By relaxing, we can become better able to see how love pervades the universe, ever so slightly hidden behind the veil of our habitual ways of seeing. Susan Piver, in *The Wisdom of a Broken Heart*, points to seemingly commonplace, everyday experiences, such as being caressed by the wind unexpectedly, as fleeting moments of intimacy with the world, "quite lovely, profound, and, if you pay attention, satisfying." Intimacy is always there, if you look for it.

This unconditional quality is called oneness, because it is not the case of two situations of being with and without love. There is no looking for love while being deprived of it, and then finding it at last, coming to a happy ending. There is only one, unconditional state. We just need to refine our perception to realize we already are in that state of being, love.

Fulfillment

Love is unconditionally present. Therefore, the situation is already fulfilled. If we have been diligent in taming our violence, pettiness, and vanity, any remaining problem will probably take care of itself. There is no need to attain anything or change anything. Love is all around, whatever the situation may be. All we need to do is relax and appreciate what there is, even (and especially) if we are heartbroken. It takes courage and conviction to see the situation as good enough, and not try to improve it.

> I want a heart torn to bits
> So that I may give a full account
> Of pain and longing.
>
> — Rumi, *Masnavi 1*

By not trying to fashion situations according to our ideas, we allow them to manifest spontaneously as they are, coming to their full measure. We are not buffeted by the ups and downs of our satisfied or unsatisfied romantic feelings. This is the only attitude that can let love be fully spontaneous. This state is full and rich. Such a fulfilled warrior is sovereign, truly in charge of his or her life.

25. The way of the samurai

The above four mysteries of love are beautifully embodied in certain elements of the wisdom of the samurai of ancient Japan: no elaborate tricks, no place for the mind, making friends with space, and a meeting of minds. This chapter attempts to discover the temperament of the consummate warrior. To approach ineffability, elusiveness, oneness, and fulfillment, the way of the samurai is spontaneous and fluid, free of any fixed form.

No elaborate tricks

Miyamoto Musashi (ca. 1584–1645) is arguably the most celebrated samurai in Japan's history. Never formally educated in the martial arts, he spent his early life as an errant swordsman, learning from the various sword schools, and fighting many duels without ever being defeated. By his own account, he did not owe his success to any superior technique, but to what he saw as a systemic weakness in the way martial arts were taught; and in his opponents, a lack of adherence to "natural principles."

At the age of 52, he became a hermit and started writing his wisdom down. He left us his *Book of Five Rings*, which is still widely read today. By the time he composed it, he had traveled and dueled extensively, and had taught many students in his own school of martial arts. He emphasized a rather small number of basic techniques, which had to be mastered thoroughly, and he denounced what he saw as the excessive number of techniques taught in other schools:

> When an excessive number of sword moves are taught, it must be to commercialize the art and impress beginners with knowledge of many moves with a sword. This attitude is to be avoided in military science.
>
> The reason for this is that it is delusion to think there are all sorts of ways of cutting people down... if there are variants, they are no more than stabbing and slashing.
> To begin with, since the point is killing, there is no reason for there to be a large number of ways to do it... In my military science, it is essential that the physical aspect and the mental state both be simple and direct...

For us, the immediate use of this insight is this: where Musashi says, *It is delusion to think there are all sorts of ways of cutting people down*, it means for us, as the Tibetan sage Longchenpa says, do not preside over an empire of possibilities. There is no time for that at all. Faced with the chaotic environment of love or war, we may want to reassure ourselves by acquiring a large number of killing methods, in the case of war. Or we may surround ourselves with a great many suitors, or make a great many plans for our existing relationship, or learn a great many bedroom or seduction tricks, in the case of love. As we saw, the proliferation of options and selection criteria is a particularly acute problem in the now-commonplace context of online dating. When we are faced with a large array of choices, be it a choice of suitors or a choice of killing methods, risking choice paralysis, we miss the point altogether:

> Generally speaking, fixation and binding are to be avoided, in both the sword and the hands. Fixation is the way to death, fluidity is the way to life. This is something that should be well understood.
>
> — *The Book of Five Rings*

Musashi goes on teaching very basic techniques along with the urging, repeated dozens of times about his various instructions: *This is something that should be well understood*, or similar wording. The emphasis throughout is not on a multiplicity of techniques, but on being calm, thorough, and mentally free. In other words, a good samurai is simple rather than contrived. And a good heart is worth a lot more than any pretension of expertise:

> What I see on inquiry into other schools is that some are pretentious talkers, and some perform fancy maneuvers with their hands; even though they may look good to people, there is surely no true heart there at all.
>
> In the science of martial arts, the state of mind should remain the same as normal. In ordinary circumstances as well as when practicing martial arts, let there be no change

at all — with the mind open and direct, neither tense nor lax, centering the mind so that there is no imbalance, relax your mind, and savor this moment of ease thoroughly so that the relaxation does not stop its relaxation for even an instant...

Generally speaking, it is essential to make your ordinary bearing the bearing you use in martial arts, and make the bearing you use in martial arts your ordinary bearing. This should be given careful consideration.

— *The Book of Five Rings*

For us aspiring lovers, it will be well if we thoroughly refrain from violence, pettiness, vanity, and agenda; and in their place cultivate their respective countering qualities. The four great enemies of love may seem as trivial to us, but they are much more pervasive than they appear. *This is something that should be well understood.*

No place for the mind

Yagyū Munenori (1571–1646) was a contemporary of Miyamoto Musashi. They had very different backgrounds. While Musashi was a self-taught and errant swordsman, Munenori learned martial arts from his father, who was well placed in the Tokugawa shogunate. He entered government service at a young age. His principal legacy is another classic, *A Hereditary Book on the Art of War*, also widely studied up to the present day. It is made of three parts, *The Killing Sword*, about the use of force; *The Life-Giving Sword*, about preventing violence; and *No Sword*, the more esoteric chapter.

Munenori and Musashi were both familiar with the philosophy of Zen, but Munenori gives it a greater part in his writings. He cites freely from his father, Yagyū Munetoshi, who also was deeply immersed in Buddhist philosophy; and also from his Zen advisor and spiritual teacher Takuan Sōhō (1573–1646). The same concern appears in their work: where to place the mind?

> Where should the mind be placed? If you place the mind on the movement of the opponent's body, your mind will be taken by the movement of the opponent's body. If you place the mind on the opponent's sword, your mind will be taken by the opponent's sword. If you place the mind on the intention to cut the opponent, your mind will be taken by the intention to cut the opponent. If you place the mind on your own sword, your mind will be taken by your own sword. If you place the mind on the thought of not being cut, your mind will be taken by the thought of not being cut. If you place the mind on the opponent's posture, your mind will be taken by the opponent's posture. In short, it is said there is no place to put the mind.
>
> — Takuan Sōhō in a letter to Yagyū Munenori

In any situation we find ourselves in, a preoccupation with an outcome or anything else robs us of our natural immediacy and spontaneity. Even the idea of being spontaneous and free of fixation is neither free nor spontaneous:

> To be fixated on the thought of winning is a disease. To be fixated on the use of sword techniques is likewise a disease. To be fixated on wanting to apply what you have learned is also a disease. To be fixated single-mindedly on attacking is a disease as well. Even to be fixated on trying to rid yourself of these very diseases is itself a disease. Here, "disease" refers to a mind that clings to one thing.
>
> — Takuan Sōhō

That is to say, at one point we need to abandon any ambition at all of accomplishing anything, even a relaxed mind free of concepts. During meditation, we can experience how thoughts and feelings arise and disappear of their own accord. Furthermore, we can also discover the futility of trying to get rid of thoughts.

> In the concluding phase, because there is no mind intent on removing the disease, the disease is removed by itself. The very mind that seeks to remove the disease becomes yet another disease. If you rest in the disease and dwell within it, you have already eliminated the disease.
>
> — Takuan Sōhō

Why is spontaneity important? The alternative is a fabricated, transparent mindset unlikely to inspire anyone at all:

> For example, when dancing, you hold a fan and move your feet. At that time, if you think about how to improve your hands and feet, your mind will naturally be drawn to your hands and feet. If your mind is drawn to them, your dancing won't be any good. When you forget your mind, your hands and feet and dancing will come naturally. When you forget your mind about anything, it is good. The more you use your mind, the worse it is.
>
> — Yagyū Munenori

There is no need to elaborate on the relevance of this wisdom to love.

Making friends with space

If we are not too caught up in the drama of our life we can see, as William Shakespeare said, that "all the world's a stage." Simply put, mind is the stage of our experience. Munenori goes on:

> The mind has no color or form, and naturally cannot be seen by the eye. However, if it becomes attached and lingers, it will inevitably become visible. It is like white

cloth: if you transfer red to it, it becomes red, and if you transfer purple to it, it becomes purple. The mind likewise will appear and become visible if it is transferred to another object. If you are intent on your opponent's movements and allow your mind to linger there, you will surely be defeated.

Our daily experience of the world of objects and phenomena is but an interpretation of an otherwise chaotic, twirling mass of clouds of electrons orbiting atomic nuclei, emitting or absorbing light as they change orbits. Besides these subatomic particles, the universe is nothing but empty space. And yet, wonder of wonders, life springs forth from that mostly empty space. Whatever meaning we ascribe to this immensity made up mostly of vacuum is a necessary expedient for us not to become insane. So it is that philosophers of various traditions (including Buddhism and Taoism, each of which influenced the way of the samurai in its own way), considered emptiness or voidness an important tenet of their worldview. The mind is a canvas, without color or shape, vast, and able to accommodate all experiences.

Past any mundane interpretation of our experience, we should not be surprised to discover, through meditation or contemplation, that our mind and our emotions are void also. For this discussion, there is no need to go into a detailed discourse of emptiness, or of existence and nonexistence. Doing the work of deep philosophers would be a lengthy distraction. The simple cloth analogy is good enough to describe the mind as the stage of one's experience. It is of no value for us to color it one way or the other, hoping to achieve some goal. Love has no characteristics that can easily be pinned down.

Do not place your mind on your opponent. The opponent is void; you yourself are void. The striking sword is void, and the hands holding the sword are also void. Finally, do not be distracted by the voidness of it all.

— Takuan Sōhō, cited by Yagyū Munenori in *Soul of the samurai*

Do not become fixated on emptiness, as that is the classic pitfall known to Mahayana Buddhists as "reifying emptiness." Takuan Sōhō warns about it, saying "do not be distracted by the voidness of it all."

The spokes of the wheel join at the hub,
Which is what makes it useful…
What exists is beneficial,
But what doesn't it truly useful.

— Tao Te Ching 11

Knowing that, we need to make friends with space. Do not project anything solid to yourself or your partner. See yourself as space, your partner as space, and your relationship as space. Of course, emptiness is not futility. It is only an absence of mental overlay. Past any notion of futility, there is no problem contemplating ourselves and our relationships as empty space, because that is also a fertile situation.

A meeting of minds

In some spiritual traditions, transmission is a meeting of minds between a teacher and a student, the acknowledgement that both teacher and student have the same potential for spiritual development. It is of interest because the mysterious qualities of oneness and fulfillment suggest a state for lovers to neither meet nor part.

AGENDA

> When two accomplished hands exchange sharp blows and there is no clear winner, it is like the time when the Buddha showed a lotus flower and Mahākāśyapa smiled. It is like knowing three things upon seeing one.
>
> — Yagyū Munenori

The above quote is cryptic, and the reference to the Buddha and Mahākāśyapa needs explaining. Again, the metaphor of combat is not the most obvious to reconcile with love. Solving a couple's quarrel should not require profundity. It is rather the notion of no clear winner that merits attention. If lovers have achieved such an exquisite balance, neither becomes dominant, and free communication takes place continuously. They are "accomplished hands" because they have overcome the obstacles that would prevent harmony between them.

This exchange between the Buddha and Mahākāśyapa is at the heart of the Sōtō Zen tradition, where enlightenment is transmitted wordlessly from teacher to disciple. In this story Mahākāśyapa, one of the Buddha's disciples, understood that wordless quality and was thus entrusted with succession:

> In front of innumerable beings on Vulture Peak, the World-Honored One [Buddha] held an udumbara blossom and blinked. The entire assembly was silent. Mahakashyapa alone broke into a smile. The World-Honored One said, "I have the treasury of the true dharma eye, the wondrous heart of nirvana. This, along with the robe [which represents succession], is entrusted to Mahakashyapa."
>
> — Dōgen, *Shōbōgenzō*

For lovers, it is the ultimate union, the absence of concept or separation of any kind. You have been together all along. With no need to say anything, you are one mind.

> Although it is not possible to fully express this principle in words, if pressed one could say that this is the point where the eyes of the Buddha and those of Kasyapa [Mahākāśyapa] become one. Like pouring water into water, water and water blend without distinction.
>
> — Takuan Sōhō in a letter to Yagyū Munenori

It is the state, not where a teacher imparts something on a student, but where both the teacher and the student realize simultaneously that they are one. It is beyond any distinction of teacher and student, of lover and beloved, to say nothing of the distinction between man and woman. The oneness of love is of the same nature as mind-to-mind transmission. We may ponder this for a long time.

> I do not say these things because I have mastered my own mind. Though I find it difficult to conduct myself, move, and remain still as if my mind were correct, or as if I had met the dictates of a correct mind, I say this because I recognize this as a state to strive for.
>
> — Yagyū Munenori

This great warrior was humble and kind enough to commit his wisdom to writing without claiming to be a master. How much humbler should we be when faced with the mystery of love? Can anyone claim to be an expert in the unknowable?

AGENDA

26. Magical practices

What can we do to develop a sense of mystery and at the same time be without agenda? The idea seems contradictory. Mystery very much consists in refraining from our habits of trying to accomplish something, of saying too much, and of trying to fill our feeling of voidness with something or other. The practices in this section help reverse those habits, so that mystery can dawn.

Aimlessness

We brush our teeth and comb our hair daily. Discipline can be as simple as that. It is not goal oriented; it is just the normal care of our life. We do not have an agenda of having our teeth brushed or our hair combed. Now perform every act in the same spirit: do everything for its own sake, as its own reward. Hindus call such selfless or desire-less activity *nishkāmakarma*, which means action performed while renouncing its fruit.

> Thy human right is for activity only, never for the resultant fruit of actions. Do not consider thyself the creator of the fruits of thy activities; neither allow thyself attachment to inactivity.
>
> O Dhananjaya (Arjuna), remaining immersed in yoga, perform all actions, forsaking attachment (to their fruits), being indifferent to success and failure. This mental evenness is termed yoga.
>
> — Bhagavad-Gītā 2:47–48

> He who gives up all desire for the fruit of his actions, renounces all activities and thus passes beyond all pairs of opposites.
>
> — Nārada Bhakti Sūtra 48

So don't try to accomplish so much. It is not all up to you. You can let the world touch you sometimes.

Plausible deniability

If you have ever engaged in courtship with anyone (whether pursuing or pursued), you may intuitively have used a device called plausible deniability. Instead of saying *I want to marry you*, or *I want to to sleep with you* (let alone *I love you*), you invite the other person to some innocuous activity, such as eating ice cream or playing at the bowling alley. Likewise when accepting or rejecting the offer, you need not mention the topic of love, sex, or marriage. While this way seems less than straightforward, it offers several advantages. In a society where violence is prevalent, or if deceit and distrust are major concerns, it is not as blunt, and may work to lower the other person's initial distrust. With regards to pettiness, this reassures the other of your propriety. It is like having good table manners. You show yourself as a respectable person, and therefore eligible, by not mentioning the unmentionable. In a social context where vanity is of great concern, you refrain from expressing too much interest in the other. Doing so, you artfully prevent this person from seeing you as unattractive:

> I know of a man whose beloved was completely friendly and at ease with him; but if he had disclosed by the least gesture that he was in love, the beloved would have become as remote as the Pleiades, whose stars hang so high in heaven. It is a sort of statesmanship that is required in such cases; the party concerned was enjoying the pleasure of his loved one's company intensely and to the last degree, but if he had so much as hinted at his inner feelings he would have attained but a miscrable fraction of

the beloved's favour, and endured into the bargain all the arrogance and caprice of which love is capable.

— Ibn Ḥazm (994–1064) in his love treatise *The Ring of the Dove*

Beyond that, practicing plausible deniability also preserves mystery, a magical quality of love and of ourselves. Not only is it not devious or underhanded, it actually makes for elegant communication:

> The way of exercising inscrutability is that you don't spell out the truth. You imply the truth, with wakeful delight in your accomplishment... When you spell out the truth you are spending your capital while no one gets any profit. It becomes undignified, a giveaway... Truth is generated from its environment; in that way it becomes a powerful reality.
>
> — Chögyam Trungpa, *Shambhala: The Sacred Path of the Warrior*

Truth is generated from its environment for us could mean *feeling* the state of being in love, and the many small acts that accompany love, rather than offering or demanding explicit assurances. You can be confident love will be expressed in countless little ways, on the strength of the situation. This should be enough to convey your message. This leaves room for each to enjoy his or her own experience, without conceptualizing it. When people come to understand one another by sharing an experience rather than through explicit communication, the situation automatically becomes magical.

To be a warrior with a broken heart

Strangely enough, our heart or mind as the empty canvas of our experience is not neutral or devoid of feeling. If we pay close attention, we may discover that every meaningful or poignant experience contains at least a tinge of sadness. To look for love and not find it is normal. Therefore to feel raw, vulnerable, and alone is normal too. We need to acknowledge that experience and become friendly with it.

Because of oneness, the experience of a broken, raw and tender heart accompanies everything. We experience this heartbreak not because of something bad that happened to us. We unconditionally have a broken heart, and we sometimes have a chance to acknowledge that. To face that heartbreak is to be a warrior. Susan Piver relates how people she interviewed remembered their own heartbreak not with bitterness, but with melancholy and a sense of sweetness:

> Although it sounds clichéd, they were grateful for the experience. I could see that, instead of considering their broken heart as extremely bad luck, they now viewed it as an experience of luminosity… They almost missed that heightened state of feeling.

Being with a broken heart is the natural state of a genuine person. From this aloneness, or vulnerability, we can relate to everyone, because this very heart of sadness is everyone's heart of hearts. We can be like an enlightened monarch in our world, caring about all in the kingdom, and able to relate with others in an authentic way:

> When you walk into this world of reality, the greater or cosmic world, you will find the way to rule your world — but, at the same time, you will also find a deep sense of aloneness. It is possible that this world could become a palace or a kingdom to you, but as its king or queen, you will be a monarch with a broken heart. It is not a bad thing

to be, by any means. In fact, it is the way to be a decent human being — and beyond that a glorious human being who can help others.

This kind of aloneness is painful, but at the same time, it is beautiful and real. Out of such painful sadness, a longing and a willingness to work with others will come naturally.

— Chögyam Trungpa, *Shambhala: The Sacred Path of the Warrior*

We can really treasure the state of having a broken heart. In order to make sense, it needs to be experienced. There is no other way.

Radical intimacy: eye gazing

Imagine having a friend or lover with whom you enjoy such a close and intimate relationship that there is no need to express your love for each other. Just being in each other's presence is enough. Because of the inherent fulfillment of love, there is no need to do anything. There are no petty cravings, furtive moves, or any kind of scheming. You can just *be* together.

According to Will Johnson's *Rumi's Four Essential Practices*, Rumi did just that with his heart friend, the wandering mystic Shams Tabrīzī. United in a deep spiritual friendship, they spent weeks and months in private retreat, apparently gazing at each other all day long, although no one knows for sure. We know that for Rumi, Shams is the *Beloved*, the embodiment of divine love. To this love, we owe Rumi's abundant and flowing verses, still widely read today. Rumi was not a poet in the ordinary sense. He spoke from a state of ecstatic spiritual rapture before his students, who noted his sayings on the spot or memorized them and later compiled them into books.

Looking into your partner's eyes does not make you less lonely. You communicate silently, becoming vulnerable, even desolate. There is always a measure of sadness and desolation. Rather than rejecting it, discovering and even embracing sadness can be a fuller way of being in love, acknowledging a deeper truth of the heart:

> Since I am intoxicated by your face, O wise sage,
> Look upon me with those drunken eyes.
> My heart twists from your drunken eyes, for it is mad—
> For the intoxicated and the mad are of the same kind.
> See my ruined heart and kindly look upon me,
> For the sun of your gaze brings joy even to a ruin.
> ...
> You have so plundered me and the house of my heart,
> That beauty itself runs barefoot through the house.
> We come to the garden of your face
>   and break down the house,
> Bravely turning a thousand houses into a desert!
>
> — Rumi, F 2412[36]

Desolation, or discovering the true taste of our heart, is in no way incompatible with the idea that authentic love is fulfilled, even sweet. The practice is as simple as it is profound. It is described by Will Johnson, a student of Rumi's eye-gazing practice. With a trusted friend or lover, find a quiet and private spot. Gaze into each other's eyes for two to four minutes at a time. This may at first seem like eternity. You may giggle. Eventually you settle, and the magic happens:

> Closer, ever closer, you feel your consciousness and energies starting to dance and commingle with your friend, until eventually you arrive at a place of such closeness and

intimacy that you realize that you don't feel separate from your friend anymore — that your soul has merged with her soul and you can no longer tell the difference.

— *Rumi's Four Essential Practices: Ecstatic Body, Awakened Soul*

As a refinement, you can touch one another lightly, holding hands or putting one hand on each other's heart, and breathe in unison.

There is also a dark side to eye gazing. Prolonged eye contact is a good way to win people over, manipulate them, and sell things to them, to say nothing of seduction. It is all too easily misused by unscrupulous politicians, con artists, and fake gurus, be they general or special. Michael Ellsberg's *Power of Eye Contact* mentions such examples of abuse. Motives can be self-serving. Gaze only with someone you trust.

27. The mysterious dragon

We have previously looked at the first three of the four dignities of the Shambhala warrior tradition: meekness, perkiness, and outrageousness. Each helped us discover an important quality of love: gentleness, grace, and charm respectively. We now turn to the fourth dignity of inscrutable warriorship, the apex of the warrior's training:

> Inscrutability is represented by the dragon. The dragon is energetic, powerful, and unwavering. But these qualities of the dragon do not stand alone without the meekness of the tiger, the perkiness of the lion, and the outrageousness of the garuda... The experience of inscrutability is not a calculating one. It is not learning a new trick nor is it

mimicking someone else. When you are at ease, you find a state of true healthy mind. The cultivation of inscrutability is to learn to be.

— Chögyam Trungpa, *Shambhala: The Sacred Path of the Warrior*

Because of this naturalness, there is no need for any scheming or elaboration. Rather, any situation a warrior encounters provides both challenge and interest, and that warrior has unconditional confidence, or confidence without object:

> It has been said that everyone possesses the potentiality to be confident. When we speak of confidence here we refer to enlightened confidence — not to confidence in something, but just to be *confident*. This confidence is unconditional. Inscrutability is a spark that is free of any analytical scheme. When meeting a situation, challenge and interest occur simultaneously. You proceed with an open mind and with direct action. This brings delight, and guidelines evolve naturally... The warrior doesn't have to struggle. A sense of struggle is not the style of inscrutability.

Since there are no special tricks or techniques, we may wonder where to begin. We are so habituated to *doing something*. This time around we may simply take the opportunity to relax instead of rushing into anything:

> The apprentice might feel impatient or inadequate. At that point you have to be inscrutable to yourself. Slowing down any impulse is said to be the best way to begin. When the warrior feels a sense of leadership and order on earth, that appreciation brings some kind of breakthrough.

By not trying to make anything happen, we allow the world to manifest as it is, alive and rich with possibilities. We do not

AGENDA

need to do anything to our world, but we may dance with it if we wish.

Contemplations

As part of a meditation session, take one of the topics below and reflect on it for a few minutes without trying to figure anything out. There are no answers to be discovered. These contemplations are meant to challenge you and help you relax your mind. When you are done, let go of all thought and feeling and meditate for a few more minutes.

Imagine all your past, present and future lovers visiting you at once, when you are on your deathbed.

Imagine loving a person of the same sex, if you are heterosexual; or of the opposite sex, if you are homosexual.

Does it matter to me personally if I never have children?

Imagine you, the world, and all living things as nothing but empty space, not as cold and dead, but teeming with life.

Is it possible for two persons to break each other's heart?

Imagine no one loves you.

When I die, what will remain of me?

I am fulfilled, with everything just as it is, at this very moment.

Consecration

In order to consecrate a new intimate relationship, you may engage in this contemplation together before the first physical act.

Imagine you are a young couple in Shambhala, the mythical enlightened kingdom. You have just married, and are sexually inexperienced. You are both sitting at the edge of the nuptial bed, beautifully clothed from the wedding, and are facing one another without touching. You are experiencing uncertainty and fullness at the same time.

This society takes sexual relations very seriously, yet says very little. The guidance it offers its young people is wise and oblique. Without anyone saying anything directly, you know that many elements have contributed to the way you came together: how you were raised, the way your families lived, how others married before you, and how you came to know each other.

It is now coming to a full circle. The causes and conditions that brought you together are unfathomable, yet you can feel society's invisible hand. It is completely wholesome, and inspires awe and confidence. There was no mistake or expedient. Everything has taken place properly. This being an enlightened society, you have seen many examples of happy families. You feel gratitude for your elders, who guided you so far, and also trusted you and respected you.

Even though this is your wedding night, it is also a very ordinary moment. Look at one another without pretense. Nothing needs to be done. Nothing needs to be revealed or explained. Everything is right here with you at this very moment. For the first time in your lives, you are permitted to one another. Open up to that reality together. Even if you do nothing else today, this alone is plenty of discovery, and plenty of sexuality.

CONSECRATION

Commentary

This contemplative practice, which aims at inviting the sacred into a new love affair, is timed precisely with this wording: *before the first physical act.* One often just drifts into sex, sometimes aided by alcohol, not wanting to be fully present. In this case, there is no pretending that lovemaking is any accident or self-indulgence. Engaging in this contemplation as a new couple before the first physical act leaves nothing ambiguous about what is happening. It is a deliberate, fearless step. Not only has nothing happened yet, so to speak, the text suggests the mere contemplation of this ripe situation is, in and of itself, *plenty of sexuality.*

This fearless state does not have to create any anxiety, because there is no need to perform any particular act. At your option, you may want to practice eye gazing for the occasion. Having fully considered sex as being a part of the relationship, in a sense the deed has already been done. There exists a similar custom among Jews, known as the *hadar yichud*, or seclusion room. In the Jewish custom, a man and a woman are not allowed to be together in seclusion unless they are married. After a wedding ceremony, the bride and groom retire for a few minutes in a separate room. This occasion is the first time when they are spending time together privately with the full sanction of society. This seclusion event occurs symbolically as part of the ceremony (or shortly after) and does not last very long. At most, the newlyweds will share a brief meal. It is the time when the marriage is said to have been consummated.

In a petty society, the consummation of the marriage has important implications because of paternity uncertainty. This may in fact be the main reason why many cultures forbid sex out of marriage. In an enlightened society, the boundary between a committed sexual relationship and a casual one also has value. Both kinds of society may have similar practices, but with different meanings. *You are permitted to one another* here does not mean any operation of law or custom, but that you have overcome the obstacles to an authentic relationship, and now acknowledge that nothing more keeps you from each other.

This society takes sexual relations very seriously, yet says very little. If normative rules of conduct are explicit and heavily insisted upon, people may rightly question their utility in love, and even rebel. That would not help. An enlightened society finds gentle, subtle, and uplifted ways of guiding its young people toward happy and conducive love affairs, lest they rebel and revert to their base instincts. *The guidance it offers its young people is wise and oblique.* Parents and elders benefit the young by setting their own examples of decency and reasonableness (which must of course include joy and a sense of humor), and especially by respecting the autonomy of individuals. Beyond that, there is not much to say by way of rules. Self-discipline is much more effective. Discipline is first and foremost an ingrained habit of wholesomeness, which covers every aspect of life. This being the case, nothing specific needs to be said about sex. Discussing sex as if it were more important than anything is out of the question. The point is not to shy away from discussion, but to preserve the mystery of love by not cluttering it with a nonessential matter. For now, contemplate your situation without unnecessary fixation on any aspect of it. Ideally, you should be equally open to having sex as to not having sex. A broad point of view is much more interesting. If desire or other emotions arise, do not follow them or suppress them. Just let them be in their natural state.

It is now coming to a full circle. A sexual union is not only subject to society's influence, enlightened or not. It also is a building block of society, a powerful force in itself. As you acknowledge your community's invisible touch and feel at peace with it, you also realize your union's power to touch and transform those around you, and all of society in turn. You feel fearless and relaxed, sovereign and ordinary all at the same time. New lovers often experience this exhilarating sense of being *on top of the world*:

> You can be completely raw and exposed with your husband or wife, your banker, your landlord, anyone you meet.
> Out of that comes an extraordinary birth: the birth of the universal monarch. The Shambhala definition of a monarch is someone who is very raw and sensitive, willing to open his or her heart to others. That is how you become a king or queen, the ruler of your world.
>
> — Chögyam Trungpa, *Shambhala: The Sacred Path of the Warrior*

Shambhala, the mythical enlightened kingdom: You may not recognize the society you live in as the one described in this contemplation. In order to reach for that primordial state of human goodness, you suspend your judgement, and for a little while pretend you actually live in this ideal world, and are a part of it. This deliberate, seeming naïveté helps relax the mind and reach for the greater vulnerability you need to relate with your partner and with the world. In this magical world, nothing other than magic brought you together. You have received magic from society, and will in turn offer the magic of your relationship. When you go back to your ordinary way of looking at society, notice how so much of the imperfection you perceive is actually your own projection. Remember that society is not external to you, but you are a component of it.

To contemplate this vast and spacious situation is to contemplate the mystery of love. By facing one another silently (or saying very little, for you are not looking for silence for its own sake), you experience an ineffable state, oneness and fulfillment, and the elusiveness of any definite conclusion. Going back to the samurai, notice there are no elaborate tricks, and there is nothing for the mind to do. There is nothing that can be figured out, and therefore the situation can be called empty, like space. And since nothing more separates you, it is a meeting of minds.

As a practical matter, you may perform this contemplation by studying the text and commentary beforehand. At the time of practice, read one paragraph at a time silently, with a few minutes' pause in between. You may find, maybe, that its four paragraphs convey gentleness, grace, charm, and mystery in turn. As your relationship matures over time, return again and again to this holistic perspective. It has the power to remind you of the mystery that brought you together in the first place.

Aspiration

The following is adapted from the four *brahmavihārā* or spiritual states (loving kindness, compassion, sympathetic joy, and equanimity) of ancient India:

May all beings be happy.
May all beings be free from suffering.
May all beings delight in each other's goodness.
May all beings enjoy the equanimity of love as oneness.

Notes

1 See for instance Archer (2000).

2 *Women "lie, cheat and steal,"* Manchester Evening News. Accessed June 27, 2025. http://www.manchestereveningnews.co.uk/news/greater-manchester-news/women-lie-cheat-and-steal-1131837.

3 For the traumatic effect on the unwilling fathers, see Knight, Kathryn. "Four men reveal the trauma of becoming a dad by deception." Mail Online. Accessed June 27, 2025. http://www.dailymail.co.uk/femail/article-2059548/Four-men-reveal-trauma-dad-deception.html.

4 Higdon (2011) and Sheldon (2001).

5 Slone and Van Slyke (2015) and Wilson (2008).

6 Klopfer (1994), Eisenberg (2005), and Hirshbein (2005).

7 Donaldson James, Susan. "Karezza, or Lovemaking Without Orgasm, Strengthens Marriages, Say Advocates." ABC News. Last modified July 10, 2012. http://abcnews.go.com/Health/karezza-lovemaking-orgasm-strengthens-marriages-advocates/story?id=16743124.

8 For a thorough research on the traditional ho'oponopono process, see the three-volume *Nānā I Ke Kumu — Look to the Source* by Pukui et. al. (1973, 1979) and Paglinawan (2020).

9 Duprée (2012)

10 Slone and Van Slyke (2015), pp. 120–1

11 Muller and Wrangham (2009), pp. 378–81

12 Muller and Wrangham (2009), pp. 11–12, 43–5 and 379.

13 Soule (2011)

14 See for instance Salon.com. "How I left the purity movement." Accessed June 26, 2025. http://www.salon.com/2014/11/02/how_i_left_the_purity_movement/.

15 Buss (2003), pp. 211–2

16 See Carothers and Reis (2013), Hyde (2005), Joel et al. (2015), and Reis and Carothers (2014). On the other hand, John Gray, a graduate of the controversial and now-defunct Columbia Pacific University, sold tens of millions of his *Men Are from Mars, Women Are from Venus* without presenting any scientific evidence. See Howarth Noonan (2007, p. 2): "While this premise is not based on established clinical and academic principles, it is an example of how incorrect and baseless ideas can displace good reasoned thinking based on research." The blatant stereotyping and the volume of sales are enough to qualify Gray's book as the bible of pettiness.

17 Rowbotham (1895), pp. 249–50

18 A number of these love cases have been recorded by Capellanus (1990), Martial d'Auvergne (1731), Raynouard (1817), and Rowbotham (1895).

19 For further exploration, refer to Saraswati (1996) or Chia (2000). For a very detailed description of the microcosmic orbit, whose benefits extends beyond sexual function, see Chia (1983).

20 This is the "lower elixir field" or *dan tian*, used in *qi gong* and in some martial arts. It usually is located about an inch and a half below the navel.

21 Singh (1993), Streeter and McBurney (2003)

22 Kenrick et al. (1990). See also Kenrick et al. (1993).

23 Penn (2003), pp. 282–3, attributes the 1899 coining of the popular phrase *conspicuous consumption* precisely to socio-sexual competition.

24 Kenrick (1989), and Kenrick et al. (1994)

25 Buss (2003), p. 178

26 "Readers Write." *Sun*, April 2012, Issue #436, Harlan, IA. The writer eventually met a man who loved her and married her durably.

27 Kirkpatrick (2006) and Bale and Archer (2013)

28 For modern footage of the ahal, see:
"Documentaire: Amaneï, touareg entre dunes et montagnes."
YouTube. Accessed November 23, 2025 (in French).
https://www.youtube.com/watch?v=WaWOunaRfH4&t=2855s.
And also:
"[Documentaire] Mano Dayak - Le Prince du désert (Touareg)."
YouTube. Accessed November 23, 2025 (in French).
https://www.youtube.com/watch?v=3bLfSobLVfY&t=960s.

29 See Benhazera (1908), pp. 32–4 and Fuchs (1956), pp. 49–52.

30 Brase and Guy (2004)

31 For a discussion toward a Hindu definition of tantra, see Wallis (2013), pp. 27–34.

32 Badiozzaman Forouzanfar's classification

33 Badiozzaman Forouzanfar's classification

34 See for instance Kramer and Alstad (1993) and Wallace (2003).

35 Higgins et al. (2012)

36 Badiozzaman Forouzanfar's classification

Index

A
Agenda, reproductive, 121, 123–144, 147, 160–161
Ahal of the Tuareg, 95–102
Aimlessness, 161
Anand, Margot, 130
Anger, 17–18, 30–31, 42
Anjali Mudra, 116
Asexual reproduction, 140–142
Asri (gallantry), 98
Attachment, 129, 138–139
Attractiveness, 79–83, 87–88, 102–103

B
Basic goodness, 104, 107–108, 113–115, 119
Beauty myth, 80, 83
Bernard de Ventadour, 59–60, 65
Bhagavad-Gita, 161
Birth control, 23, 26–27, 137
Bismarck, Otto von, 4
Broken heart, warrior with, 139, 163–165
Buddha, 11, 17, 31, 158–160
Buddhism, 3, 5–6, 42, 54–55, 146, 157–159
Buss, David, 5–6, 41, 44–45, 79–80, 146

C
Calhoun, John, 22
Capellanus, Andreas, 59
Celibacy, 21–25
Charm, 2–3, 77, 89–90, 105–108, 114, 128
Chia, Mantak, 4–5, 119
Chinese medicine, 32, 70–72, 127–128
Choice paralysis, 136–137, 152
Compassion, 52–54, 107
Competition, 81–83, 87, 103
Confidence, unconditional, 104, 107–108, 168
Consecration, 171–175
Constancy, 60

Contemplations, 34, 75, 120, 170
Courtly love, 56–67, 89, 94–95, 128

D
Dalai Lama, 14, 17, 24, 53
Darwin, Charles, 79, 84
Deception, 12, 15–16, 46–47, 130–131
Diversity, law of, 142–144
Divorce, 12, 50, 86
Dōgen, 159
Dragon, inscrutable, 146, 167–169
Drama, 45–46

E
Ego, 124–125, 131, 139
Ejaculation, withholding, 4–5, 25–27, 73
Elusiveness, 149
Emptiness, 125, 157–158
Enlightenment, 108–113, 118
Evolutionary psychology, 5–6, 40–42, 53, 79–83
Exclusivity, 59–60
Exploitation, 48
Eye gazing, 165–167

F
Family courts, 12–13, 50
Fear, 125–127
Feuerstein, Georg, 109
Finkel, Eli J., 83, 134–136
Forgiveness, 27–31
Frantzis, Bruce Kumar, 73
Fromm, Erich, 136, 147
Futility, 137

G
Gandhi, M.K., 7, 14–16, 20
Garuda, 105–108
Garuda's breath, 104
Gender roles, 49–51, 72
Gentleness, 2, 14–16, 25, 32–33, 107

179

Giving and receiving, 54–56
Goodness, see Basic goodness
Grace, 2–3, 37, 52, 73–74, 107
Guru, becoming a, 132–134

H
Haertig, Dr., 28
Hawaiian culture, 27–31, 114
Heartbreak, 137–139, 163–165
Ho'oponopono, 27–31
Homosexuality, 48–49, 72, 140
Hypocrisy, 48–49

I
Ibn 'Arabi, 144
Ibn Hazm, 162
Ineffability, 148
Infatuation, 46–47, 65, 127
Inscrutability, 167–169
Intercourse, 25–27, 70–73, 115–119

J
Jealousy, 42–45, 53, 75, 98, 126
Jesus, 131
Johnson, Will, 165–166

K
Kama Sutra, 85, 112
Karezza, 26–27, 70, 117, 119
Kenrick, Douglas T., 81–82
Kindness, 17, 53, 107
Kissing, 68–70

L
Lauzengier, 66
Lawrence, D.H., 149
Lorenz, Konrad, 22
Love, conditional vs. unconditional, 126–127, 148–150
Love, courts of, 56–58, 66–67
Love, four mysteries of, 147–151
Lovemaking, 25–27, 70–73, 115–119

M
Magic, sexual, 130–132
Mahākāśyapa, 158–160
Malamuth, Neil, 11
Marriage, 12, 43, 60, 81–82, 129–130
Marx, Groucho, 82
Masters, William and Johnson, Virginia, 25
Mate retention, 44–45, 47
Mediocrity, 46–47
Meditation, 17–19, 54–55, 104, 155
Meekness, 32–33
Microcosmic orbit, 70–73, 117
Mind, placing the, 154–156
Mindfulness, 17–19
Moller, Herbert, 61–62, 89, 94
Monarchy, universal, 164, 174
Musashi, Miyamoto, 151–154
Mystery, 2–3, 121, 145–170

N
Namaste, 116, 118
Narada Bhakti Sutra, 148, 161
Neo–Tantrism, 109
Nhât Hạnh, Thích, 18, 106
Nishkāmakarma, 161
Nonviolence, 14–16, 21, 27–28, 63
Nonviolent communication, 19–21

O
Objectification, 134–137
Obsession, 88–89, 137–138
Online dating, 134–137, 152
Oneness, 149–150, 158–160, 164
Orgasm, 25–27, 73, 109, 118–119
Osho, 110, 130
Outrageousness, 105–108

P
Padmasambhava, 111
Paul the Apostle, 23–24

PC muscle, 70–71
Peacock, problem of, 84–87, 102–104, 108, 115
Percentiles, law of, 87–90, 95, 117, 138
Perkiness, 73–74
Pettiness, 2, 37, 39–52, 107, 123, 126
Pickup artists, 70, 82, 91–93, 112, 138
Piver, Susan, 129, 149, 164
Plausible deniability, 162–163
Pledge, 35
Pope Francis, 87
Population, 22–23, 24
Possessiveness, 42–45

Q
Qur'an, 17

R
Randolph, Paschal B., 130–131
Rape, 11–12, 20
Reciprocity, 61–63
Reproduction, 22–25, 32, 40, 130, 139–144
Rosenberg, Marshall, 19–21
Rumi, 123, 125, 132–133, 138–139, 150, 165–166

S
Samurai, way of, 146, 151–160, 175
Seduction, 112, 128–129, 132–133, 138, 167
Self–abasement, 45, 47, 54, 61
Self–delusion, 46–47
Self–esteem, 87–88, 91, 103–104
Sex, casual, 20, 22
Sex, purpose of, 139–144
Sexual magic, 130–132
Sexual selection, 84, 142
Shakespeare, William, 156
Shambhala tradition, 3, 5, 16, 32–33, 73–74, 105–108, 146, 167–169, 171, 174
Simeona, Morrnah Nalamaku, 29
Sincerity, 60

Snow lion, 73–74
Sōhō, Takuan, 118, 154–155, 157–158, 160
Spirituality, 4–6, 13, 16–17, 24, 108–115, 124–125, 131
Spontaneity, 64, 102, 128, 146, 155–156
Stockham, Alice B., 26
Stonewalling, 45–46

T
Takuan Sōhō, see Sōhō, Takuan
Tantra, 108–115, 117–118, 133
Tao Te Ching, 115, 134, 158
Thorn, Clarisse, 68, 85
Tiger, poise of, 32–33
Tonglen, 54–56
Transmission, 158–160
Troubadours, 59–60, 63–66, 94–95
Trungpa, Chögyam, 11, 16, 33, 74, 106–107, 110, 124–125, 127, 131, 133, 145, 163, 165, 168, 174
Tuareg, 95–102

U
Unconditional love, 126–127, 143, 148–150

V–Z
Vajroli mudra, 70
Vanity, 2, 77, 79–90, 100, 102–108, 114, 116–117, 123, 126, 142, 144
Vijñāna Bhairava Tantra, 110–111
Violence, 2, 9, 11–15, 20–21, 88, 107, 123, 126
Virginity, 49, 98
Vivekananda, Swami, 113
Wilson, Edward O., 140–141
Wolf, Naomi, 80, 83
Wrangham, Richard, 15
Yagyū Munenori, 154–156, 158–160
Yin and yang, 71–72, 118
Zen Buddhism, 146, 154, 159

Bibliography

Anand, Margot. *The Art of Sexual Magic*. New York: Putnam, 1996.

Archer, John. "Sex differences in aggression between heterosexual partners: A meta-analytic review." *Psychological Bulletin* 126, no. 5 (2000): 651–80.

Bale, Christopher, and John Archer. "Self-perceived attractiveness, romantic desirability and self-esteem: A mating sociometer perspective." *Evolutionary Psychology* 11, no. 1 (2013): 68–84.

Barkow, Jerome H., Leda Cosmides, and John Tooby. "The Evolution of Sexual Attraction: Evaluative Mechanisms in Women." In *The Adapted Mind: Evolutionary Psychology and the Generation of Culture*. New York: Oxford University Press, 1992.

Baskerville, Stephen. *Taken into Custody: The War against Fathers, Marriage, and the Family*. Nashville, Tenn: Cumberland House, 2007.

Beer, Robert. *The Handbook of Tibetan Buddhist Symbols*. Boston: Shambhala, 2003.

Benhazera, Maurice. *Six mois chez les Touareg du Ahaggar*. [Six months with the Tuareg of the Hoggar] Algiers: A. Jourdan, 1908.

Beyer, Stephan V. *The Cult of Tārā: Magic and Ritual in Tibet*. Berkeley: University of California Press, 1978.

Brase, Gary L., and Emma C. Guy. "The demographics of mate value and self-esteem." *Personality and Individual Differences* 36, no. 2 (2004): 471–484.

Buss, David M. "From vigilance to violence: Tactics of mate retention in American undergraduates." *Ethology and Sociobiology* 9 (1988): 291–317. doi:10.1016/0162-3095(88)90010-6.

Buss, David M. "Sex Differences in Human Mate Preferences: Evolutionary Hypotheses Tested in 37 Cultures." *Behavioral and Brain Sciences*, 1989. doi:10.1017/S0140525X00023992.

Buss, David M. *The Evolution of Desire: Strategies of Human Mating.* New York: Basic Books, 2003.

Buss, David M., Todd K. Shackelford, and William F. McKibbin. "The Mate Retention Inventory—Short Form (MRI-SF)." *Personality and Individual Differences* (2008): doi:10.1016/j.paid.2007.08.013.

Calhoun, John B. "Population density and social pathology." *Scientific American* 206, no. 3 (1962): 139–148.

Capellanus, Andreas. *The Art of Courtly Love.* New York: Columbia University Press, 1990.

Carothers, Bobbi J., and Harry T. Reis. "Men and women are from Earth: Examining the latent structure of gender." *Journal of Personality and Social Psychology* 104, no. 2 (2013): 385.

Castaneda, Carlos. *The Teachings of Don Juan; A Yaqui Way of Knowledge.* Berkeley: University of California Press, 1968.

Chia, Mantak. *Awaken Healing Energy Through the Tao: The Taoist Secret of Circulating Internal Power.* New York, N.Y.: Aurora Press, 1983.

Chia, Mantak. *The Multi-Orgasmic Couple: Sexual Secrets Every Couple Should Know.* San Francisco: Harper San Francisco, 2000.

Chia, Mantak, and Maneewan Chia. *Healing Love Through the Tao: Cultivating Female Sexual Energy.* Huntington, N.Y.: Healing Tao Books, 1986.

Chia, Mantak, and Michael Winn. *Taoist Secrets of Love: Cultivating Male Sexual Energy.* New York, N.Y.: Aurora Press, 1984.

Cleary, Thomas F., Munenori Yagyū, and Takuan Sōhō. *Soul of the samurai.* North Clarendon, Vt: Tuttle Pub, 2005.

Dōgen, Kazuaki Tanahashi. *Treasury of the True Dharma Eye : Zen Master Dogen's Shobo Genzo. Vol. 2.* Boston: Shambhala, 2010.

Duprée, Ulrich Emil, and Tony Mitton. *Ho'oponopono: The Hawaiian Forgiveness Ritual As the Key to Your Life's Fulfillment.* Forres, Scotland: Earthdancer, 2012.

Eisenberg, Leon. Which Image for Lorenz? *American Journal of Psychiatry* 162, no. 9 (2005): 1760. doi:10.1176/appi.ajp.162.9.1760.

Ellsberg, Michael. *The Power of Eye Contact: Your Secret for Success in Business, Love, and Life*. New York: HarperCollins, 2010.

Feuerstein, Georg. *Tantra: The Path of Ecstasy*. Boston: Shambhala, 1998.

Finkel, Eli J., and Paul W. Eastwick. "Arbitrary Social Norms Influence Sex Differences in Romantic Selectivity." *Psychological Science* 20.10 (2009): 1290–5.

Finkel, Eli J., Paul W. Eastwick, Benjamin R. Karney, Harry T. Reis, and Susan Sprecher. "Online Dating A Critical Analysis From the Perspective of Psychological Science." *Psychological Science in the Public Interest* 13.1 (2012): 3–66.

Frantzis, Bruce Kumar. *Opening the Energy Gates of Your Body: Chi Gung for Lifelong Health*. Berkeley: Blue Snake, 2006.

Fromm, Erich. *The Art of Loving*. New York: Harper & Row, 1962.

Frost, Jeana H., et al. "People are experience goods: Improving online dating with virtual dates." *Journal of Interactive Marketing* 22.1 (2008): 51–61.

Fuchs, Peter. *The Land of Veiled Men*. New York: Citadel Press, 1956.

Gates, Barbara, and Wes Nisker. "Advice from the Dalai Lama," by Jack Kornfield. In *The Best of Inquiring Mind: Twenty-Five Years of Dharma, Drama, & Uncommon Insight*, 55. Boston: Wisdom Publications, 2008.

Gersi, Douchan. *La dernière grande aventure des Touareg*. [The Tuareg's last great adventure] Paris: Robert Laffont, 1972.

Goettner-Abendroth, Heide. *Matriarchal Societies: Studies on Indigenous Cultures Across the Globe Revised Edition*. Peter Lang International Academic Publishers, 2013.

Gray, John. *Men Are from Mars, Women Are from Venus: A Practical Guide for Improving Communication and Getting What You Want in Your Relationships*. New York: HarperCollins, 1992.

Higdon, Michael J. "Fatherhood by conscription: Nonconsensual insemination and the duty of child support." *Georgia Law Review* 46 (2011): 407.

Higgins, J. A., Popkin, R. A., & Santelli, J. S. (2012). Pregnancy ambivalence and contraceptive use among young adults in the United States. *Perspectives on Sexual and Reproductive Health*, 44(4), 236–43.

Hirshbein, Laura D. Dr. Hirshbein Replies. *American Journal of Psychiatry* 162, no. 9 (2005): 1760. doi:10.1176/appi.ajp.162.9.1760.

Hosmanek, Andrew J. "Cutting the Cord: Ho'oponopono and Hawaiian Restorative Justice in the Criminal Law Context." *SSRN Electronic Journal*, 2004. doi:10.2139/ssrn.635863.

Howarth Noonan, Jo. "Men are from Mars, Women are from Venus: An Analysis of a Potential Meme." Master's thesis, Georgia State University, 2007.

Hyde, Janet Shibley. "The gender similarities hypothesis." *American psychologist* 60.6 (2005): 581.

Ibn Ḥazm, *The Ring of the Dove*. London: Luzac & Co., 1953.

Jalāl al-Dīn Rūmī. *Mystical Poems: First Selection, Poems 1–200*. Chicago: University of Chicago Press, 1969.

Jalāl al-Dīn Rūmī. *Mystical Poems of Rūmī: Second Selection, Poems 201–400*. Boulder: Westview Press, 1979.

Joel, Daphna, Zohar Berman, Ido Tavor, Nadav Wexler, Olga Gaber, Yaniv Stein, Nisan Shefi et al. "Sex beyond the genitalia: The human brain mosaic." *Proceedings of the National Academy of Sciences* (2015): 201509654.

Johnson, Will. *Rumi's Four Essential Practices: Ecstatic Body, Awakened Soul*. Rochester, VT: Inner Traditions, 2010.

Kenrick, D. "Influence of Popular Erotica on Judgments of Strangers and Mates." *Journal of Experimental Social Psychology*, 1989. doi:10.1016/0022-1031(89)90010-3.

Kenrick, Douglas T., Edward K. Sadalla, Gary Groth, and Melanie R. Trost. "Evolution, Traits, and the Stages of Human Courtship: Qualifying the Parental Investment Model." *Journal of Personality*, 1990. doi:10.1111/j.1467-6494.1990.tb00909.x.

Kenrick, Douglas T., Gary E. Groth, Melanie R. Trost, and Edward K. Sadalla. "Integrating evolutionary and social exchange perspectives on relationships: Effects of gender, self-appraisal, and involvement level on mate selection criteria." *Journal of Personality and Social Psychology* 64, no. 6 (1993), 951-969. doi:10.1037//0022-3514.64.6.951.

Kenrick, D. T., S. L. Neuberg, K. L. Zierk, and J. M. Krones. "Evolution and Social Cognition: Contrast Effects As a Function of Sex, Dominance, and Physical Attractiveness." *Personality and Social Psychology Bulletin*, 1994. doi:10.1177/0146167294202008.

Kirkpatrick, Lee A., and Bruce J. Ellis. "What is the evolutionary significance of self-esteem? The adaptive functions of self-evaluative psychological mechanisms." *Self-esteem: Issues and answers* (2006): 334–339.

Klopfer, Peter. *Konrad Lorenz and the National Socialists: On the Politics of Ethology*. International Journal of Comparative Psychology. eScholarship, University of California, 1994.

Kramer, Joel, and Diana Alstad. *The Guru Papers: Masks of Authoritarian Power*. Berkeley: North Atlantic Books/Frog, 1993.

Landaw, Jonathan. *Prince Siddhartha: The Story of Buddha*. Somerville, MA: Wisdom Publications, 2003.

Laozi, Witter Bynner. *The way of life according to Lao-Tzu*. New York: Perigee, 1962.

Lawrence, David Herbert, and Christopher Pollnitz. *The Poems. Volume I*. Cambridge: Cambridge University press, 2013.

Lhote, Henri. *Les Touaregs du Hoggar*, 2nd ed. [The Tuareg of the Hoggar] Paris: Payot, 1955.

Lorenz, Konrad. *On Aggression*. New York: Harcourt, Brace & World, 1966.

Malamuth, Neil M. "Rape Proclivity Among Males." *Journal of Social Issues* 37, no. 4 (1981): 138–57.

Martial d'Auvergne. *Les Arrêts d'Amours: avec L'Amant rendu Cordelier, à l'Observance D'amours*. Amsterdam, Paris: Pierre Gandouin, 1731.

Masters, William H., and Virginia E. Johnson. *Human Sexual Response*. Boston: Little, Brown and Company, 1966.

Maull, Fleet. *Dharma in Hell: The Prison Writings of Fleet Maull*. Boulder: Prison Dharma Network, 2005.

Miyamoto Musashi, Thomas F. Cleary, and Yagyū Munenori. *The Book of Five Rings*. Boston: Shambhala, 1993.

Moller, Herbert. "The Social Causation of the Courtly Love Complex." Comparative Studies in Society and History (1959): doi:10.1017/S0010417500000177, pp. 137–163.

Muller, Martin N., and Richard W. Wrangham. *Sexual Coercion in Primates and Humans: An Evolutionary Perspective on Male Aggression against Females*. Cambridge: Harvard University Press, 2009.

Mystery, Chris Odom. *The Mystery Method: How to Get Beautiful Women into Bed*. New York, N.Y.: St. Martin's Press, 2007.

Nhât Hạnh, Arnold Kotler. *Peace Is Every Step: The Path of Mindfulness in Everyday Life*. New York, N.Y.: Bantam Books, 1991.

Odier, Daniel. *Tantra yoga: le Vijñânabhaïrava tantra, le "tantra de la connaissance suprême."* Paris: Albin Michel, 2004.

Padmasambhava, Kennard Lipman tr. *Secret teachings of Padmasambhava: essential instructions on mastering the energies of life*. Boston: Shambhala, 2010.

Paige, Glenn D., and Sarah Gilliatt. *Nonviolence in Hawaii's Spiritual Traditions*. Honolulu, Hawaii: Center for Global Nonviolence Planning Project, Spark M. Matsunaga Institute for Peace, University of Hawaii, 1991.

Pema Chödrön. *Start Where You Are: A Guide to Compassionate Living*. Boston: Shambhala, 1994.

Pema Chödrön and Tingdzin Ötro. *Tonglen: The Path of Transformation*. Halifax: Vajradhatu Publications, 2001.

Penn, Dustin J. "The Evolutionary Roots of Our Environmental Problems: Toward a Darwinian Ecology." *Quarterly Review of Biology*, 2003. doi:10.1086/377051.

Piver, Susan. *The Wisdom of a Broken Heart: How to Turn the Pain of a Breakup into Healing, Insight, and New Love*. New York: Free Press, 2011.

Paglinawan, Lynette K., Richard L. Paglinawan, Dennis Kauahi, and Valli K. Kanuha. *Nānā I Ke Kumu: Helu 'Ekolu (Look to the Source) Vol. 3*. Honolulu: Lili'upkalani Trust, 2020.

Pukui, Mary K., E. W. Haertig, and Catherine A. Lee. *Nānā i Ke Kumu (Look to the Source) Vol. 1*. Honolulu: Hui Hanai, 1973.

Pukui, Mary K., E. W. Haertig, and Catharine A. Lee. *Nānā I Ke Kumu (Look to the Source) Vol. 2*. Honolulu: Hui Hanai, 1979.

Randolph, Paschal Beverly, Maria de Naglowska, and Donald Traxler. *Magia Sexualis: Sexual Practices for Magical Power*. Rochester, VT: Inner Traditions, 2012.

Raynouard, François J. M. *Des troubadours et des cours d'amour*. Paris: Imprimerie de Fernand Didot, 1817.

Reis, Harry T., and Bobbi J. Carothers. "Black and White or Shades of Gray Are Gender Differences Categorical or Dimensional?." *Current Directions in Psychological Science* 23, no. 1 (2014): 19–26.

Ronay, R., and W. V. Hippel. "The Presence of an Attractive Woman Elevates Testosterone and Physical Risk Taking in Young Men." *Social Psychological and Personality Science* (2010): doi:10.1177/1948550609352807.

Rowbotham, John Frederick. *The Troubadours and Courts of Love*. New York: MacMillan & Co., 1895.

Rosenberg, Marshall B. *Nonviolent Communication: A Language of Life*. Encinatas: PuddleDancer Press, 2003.

Rosenberg, Samuel N., Margaret Louise Switten, Gérard Le Vot, Peter Becker, and Robert Eisenstein. *Songs of the troubadours and trouvères: an anthology of poems and melodies.* 1998.

Saraswati, Sunyata. *Jewel in the Lotus: The Tantric Path to Higher Consciousness.* Taos, NM: Tantrika International, Sunstar Pub, 1996.

Sarma, Y. Subrahmanya. *Narada's Aphorisms on Bhakti.* Holenasipur: Adhyatma Prakasha Karyalaya, 1938.

Schnell, Rüdiger. "L'amour courtois en tant que discours courtois sur l'amour." [Courtly love as a courtly discourse on love] *Romania* 110 (1989): 73–126, 331–363.

Shaw, Miranda Eberle. *Passionate Enlightenment: Women in Tantric Buddhism.* Princeton, NJ: Princeton University Press, 1994.

Sheldon, Sally. "'Sperm bandits,' birth control fraud and the battle of the sexes." *Legal Studies* 21, no. 3 (2001): 460–80.

Singh, Devendra. "Adaptive Significance of Female Physical Attractiveness: Role of Waist-to-hip Ratio." *Journal of Personality and Social Psychology,* 1993. doi:10.1037//0022-3514.65.2.293.

Singh, Jaideva. *Vijñānabhairava or Divine Consciousness: a treasury of 112 types of Yoga: Sanskrit text with English translation, expository notes, introduction and glossary of technical terms.* Delhi: Motilal Banarsidass, 2006.

Slone ed., Jason, and James Van Slyke ed. "When Religion Makes it Worse: Religiously-Motivated Violence as a Sexual Selection Weapon." In *The Attraction of Religion: A New Evolutionary Psychology of Religion.* London: Bloomsbury Academic, 2015.

Soho, T. *The unfettered mind: Writings from a Zen master to a master swordsman.* Boston: Shambhala, 2012.

Soule, Kari P. "The What, When, Who and Why of Nagging in Interpersonal Relationships." In *Making Connections: Readings in Relational Communication,* 5th ed. New York: Oxford University Press, 2011.

Steinilber-Oberlin, Émile. *Les Touareg tels que je les ai vus : Au cœur du Hoggar mystérieux*. [The Tuareg as I saw them: In the heart of the mysterious Hoggar] Paris: Ed. Pierre Roger, 1934.

Stockham, Alice B. *Karezza, Ethics of Marriage*. Forgotten Books, 2008. First published in 1903.

Strauss, Neil. *The Stylelife Challenge: Master the Game in 30 Days*. New York: Harper, 2007.

Streeter, Sybil A., and Donald H. McBurney. "Waist-hip ratio and attractiveness: New evidence and a critique of a 'critical test'." *Evolution and Human Behavior*, no. 24 (2003): 88–98.

Thompson, Robert Farris. *Aesthetic of the Cool: Afro-Atlantic Art and Music*. Pittsburgh: Periscope Publishing, 2011.

Thorn, Clarisse. *Confessions of a Pickup Artist Chaser: Long Interviews with Hideous Men*. Charleston, SC: CreateSpace, 2012.

Traleg Kyabgon. *The Practice of Lojong: Cultivating Compassion Through Training the Mind*. Boston: Shambhala, 2007.

Trungpa, Chögyam, and John Baker. *Cutting Through Spiritual Materialism*. Berkeley: Shambhala, 1973.

Trungpa, Chögyam. *Shambhala: The Sacred Path of the Warrior*. Boston: Shambhala, 1984.

Trungpa, Chögyam, and Sherab Chödzin. *Crazy Wisdom*. Boston: Shambhala, 1991.

Trungpa, Chögyam, and Judith L. Lief. *Training the Mind and Cultivating Loving-Kindness*. Boston: Shambhala, 1993.

Trungpa, Chögyam. *The Collected Works of Chögyam Trungpa: Crazy wisdom ; Illusion's game : the life and teachings of Naropa ; The life of Marpa the translator (excerpts) ; The rain of wisdom (excerpts)*. Boulder: Shambhala Publications, 2003.

Trungpa, Chögyam, and Judith L. Lief. *True Perception: The Path of Dharma Art*. Boston: Shambhala, 2008.

Urban, Hugh B. *Magia Sexualis Sex, Magic, and Liberation in Modern Western Esotericism.* Berkeley: University of California Press, 2006.

Vātsyāyana, Richard Francis Burton, and F. F. Arbuthnot. *The Kama Sutra of Vatsyayana: The Classic Hindu Treatise on Love and Social Conduct.* Bombay: Jaico Pub. House, 1963.

Vitale, Joe, and Ihaleakala H. Len. *Zero Limits: The Secret Hawaiian System for Wealth, Health, Peace, and More.* Hoboken: John Wiley & Sons, 2008.

Vivekānanda. *The Complete Works of Swami Vivekananda: Mayavati Memorial Edition Volume 3.* Calcutta: Advaita Ashrama, 1973.

Wallace, Amy. *Sorcerer's Apprentice: My Life with Carlos Castaneda.* Berkeley: Frog, 2003.

Wallis, Christopher D. *Tantra Illuminated: The Philosophy, History, and Practice of a Timeless Tradition.* Boulder: Mattamayūra Pr., 2013.

Wilson, Christopher G. "Male genital mutilation: an adaptation to sexual conflict." *Evolution and Human Behavior* 29 (2008): 149–164. doi:10.1016/j.evolhumbehav.2007.11.008.

Wilson, Edward O. *On Human Nature.* Cambridge: Harvard University Press, 1978.

Wolf, Naomi. *The Beauty Myth: How Images of Beauty Are Used against Women.* New York: Perennial, 2002.

Wrangham, Richard W., and Dale Peterson. *Demonic Males: Apes and the Origins of Human Violence.* Boston: Houghton Mifflin, 1996.

Yagyū Munenori. *The Sword and the Mind.* Woodstock, N.Y.: Overlook Press, 1985.

Yang, Martin C. *A Chinese Village: Taitou, Shantung Province.* New York: Columbia University Press, 1965.

Yogananda. *The Bhagavad Gita: God Talks with Arjuna: Royal Science of God-Realization: Chapters 1–5.* Los Angeles: Self Realization Fellowship, 2001.

www.ingramcontent.com/pod-product-compliance
Lightning Source LLC
Chambersburg PA
CBHW020614300426
44113CB00007B/634